TANTRIC SEXUALITY

 a beginner's guide

RICHARD CRAZE

Hodder & Stoughton

A MEMBER OF THE HODDER HEADLINE GROUP

This book is dedicated to Roni Jay and Quarterstaff – with love

ABOUT THE AUTHOR

Richard Craze is a full-time writer specialising in books on religion, Chinese culture, sex and esoteric subjects. His other books include:

Graphology for Beginners (Hodder & Stoughton, 1994)

Feng Shui for Beginners (Hodder & Stoughton, 1995)

Chinese Herbal Medicine (Piatkus, 1995)

The Spiritual Traditions of Sex (Godsfield Press, UK, 1996)

Teach Yourself the Alexander Technique (Hodder & Stoughton, 1996)

The Card Playing Kit (Simon & Schuster, Australia, 1995)

Astral Projection – A Beginner's Guide (Hodder & Stoughton, 1996)

Hell – An Illustrated History of the Netherworld (Conari, USA, 1996)

The Feng Shui Pack (Godsfield Press, UK, 1997)

Order queries: please contact Bookpoint Ltd, 39 Milton Park, Abingdon, Oxon OX14 4TD. Telephone: (44) 01235 400414, Fax: (44) 01235 400454. Lines are open from 9.00–6.00, Monday to Saturday, with a 24-hour message answering service. Email address: orders@bookpoint.co.uk

British Library Cataloguing in Publication Data
A catalogue record for this title is available from The British Library

ISBN 0 340 74246 1

First published 1997
This edition published 1999
Impression number 10 9 8 7 6 5 4 3 2 1
Year   2004 2003 2002 2001 2000 1999

Typeset by Transet Limited, Coventry, England.
Printed in Great Britain for Hodder & Stoughton Educational, a division of Hodder Headline plc, 338 Euston Road, London NW1 3BH by Cox and Wyman Limited, Reading, Berks.

CONTENTS

Chapter 9   The spirituality of the erotic   93

Useful information   102

ᴅɪsᴄʟᴀɪᴍᴇʀ

Although all the exercises and techniques you will find in this book are perfectly safe, the author and publishers cannot be held responsible for any accident or injury that may befall readers if they choose to try them. Whilst we are confident that there is nothing in this book that could be harmful or injurious we have no control over the health or fitness of our readers. Therefore we would advise that if you have any doubt about your own suitability to try anything in this book you should consult a qualified medical practitioner.

INTRODUCTION

O you men, one and all, who are soliciting the love of woman and her affection, and who wish that sentiment in her heart to be of an enduring nature, play with her previous to intercourse; prepare her for enjoyment, and neglect nothing to attain that end. Explore her with the greatest care, and entirely occupied with her, let nothing else engage your thoughts. Do not let the moment best for pleasure pass away; that moment will be when you see her eyes moist, half closed. Then go to work, but remember, not until your kisses and playing have taken effect.

The Perfumed Garden

What is tantric sex?

The word 'tantric' comes from the Indian *tantra* which means a written text. These texts were known as threads or fundamentals because their subject matter invariably concerned important issues such as sex, religion or the attainment of enlightenment. A tantra was the written equivalent to a *mantra*, a spoken chant or prayer which could bring about a union with God if used correctly and repeatedly. Likewise a *yantra* was a drawing or painting, usually geometric, that could achieve a similar result if studied hard enough or meditated upon.

Sex manuals

The most famous tantric books are the Indian *Kama Sutra* and the *Ananga Ranga*, the Arabic *Perfumed Garden*, the Chinese 'pillow books' such as the *T'ung Hsuan Tzu* (Tao of Sex) and the Japanese *Shunga* ('spring drawings'). You may have heard of some if not all of these, but how many of you have actually read them? To be honest they're quite hard going. They were written a long time ago and have lost a lot both through translation and through the differences in culture. But we must be careful not to dismiss them as antiquated and irrelevant texts that couldn't possibly have any bearing on our modern lives or be of any use to us. They do contain, often hidden in flowery or esoteric language, a vast wealth of practical, unusual and fascinating information about how we can improve our sex lives, alter the focus of our lovemaking and find a new satisfaction within a committed and lasting relationship.

Different forms of tantrism

Tantric sex has followed many different paths; there have been tantric Buddhists, tantric Hindus, tantric Taoists and even tantric agnostics. They invariably, albeit to differing degrees, use sex as a focus for channelling energy towards a higher or more spiritual end. In this book you will find a unique distillation of all the best techniques and practical exercises from the tantric texts of the past. There is no pressure to follow any particular path, nor is there any attempt to encourage you to do anything you may find difficult or for which you have any hesitation. Any of the exercises and techniques you will find in the following chapters are given for your information – try as many or as few as you like. Those that you enjoy or help you achieve a specific result you can keep; those that you don't like or find unsatisfactory you can abandon without a second thought.

Sex is an intensely personal experience and what suits one couple may be unhelpful to another. Feel free also to experiment, to take exercises further, to invent your own, to adapt, modify, change or

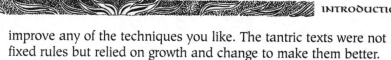

improve any of the techniques you like. The tantric texts were not fixed rules but relied on growth and change to make them better. Likewise you can learn only by trial and error.

The four Aims of the Hindus

The original tantric way was probably Hindu. The Hindus believed that there was a four-way path towards enlightenment. The first was *dharma* – following correct social and moral behaviour; this obviously varied depending on what caste you were or what profession you followed. The second of the Aims was *artha* – material wealth and comfort. The third was *kama* – love and physical pleasure. And the fourth was enlightenment itself – *kaivalya* – brought about by following the first three. We are interested in this book in the third of the Four Aims which is kama. All of the Aims had various texts written about them which are known as the *sutras*, or philosophies. Hence the *Kama Sutra* - the philosophy of love and physical pleasure – which we will look at more closely in later chapters.

Sex as religious worship

The fact that the Hindus saw both material wealth and pleasure as being pathways to enlightenment often surprises or even shocks people from the West. The ancient religions of India, Arabia and China saw comfort, food, drink and sex as being not only essential parts of the human psyche but also as unsuppressable urges. If they could not be suppressed then they should be put to good use; to be perfected and used as a focus for a higher or more spiritual life. The Hindus also saw human life as holistic – there was no division between religion and everyday life. Every duty, every task, every indulgence could be carried out as a religious act of worship so that you didn't have to make a specific time or place for worship but could incorporate it into every facet of your life.

It makes sense to include God in your daily life within every activity rather than excluding the Divine until you're ready to pick it up again – after all, it is with us constantly anyway. The tantric practitioners were merely acknowledging that which we all know – that there is no separation. Not only were they acknowledging it, they were using it to enjoy their lives and increase their opportunities to move forwards on the four-fold path.

The Kama Sutra

About two thousand years ago an Indian aristocrat and wise man, Vatsyayana, collected the best of the Hindu erotic manuals around at that time and edited them into one volume – the *Kama Sutra*. It was translated into English in the 1860s by Sir Richard Burton, an Indian Army Officer and, as you can imagine for its time, caused a considerable stir in the West. Nobody had ever seen anything quite like it and it generated an enormous amount of controversy – was it pornography or education? Various members of the Church declared it ungodly and demanded its immediate destruction. Luckily for us it survived.

This book is not only a sex manual as we would think of it in modern terms but a guide to the right foods to eat before lovemaking, the right style of courtship, a recipe book of aphrodisiacs, an instruction guide for making love charms, a keep fit and exercise manual, a marriage guidance advice book, and even a travel guide with advice on where to meet girls, how to avoid contagious diseases and the best places to buy sex aids.

Many people believe that the *Kama Sutra* is merely a collection of bizarre sexual positions but it is much, much more. It includes discussions on health and marriage, how to attract a partner, how to avoid adultery, sensual and arousing kissing, embracing and very erotic foreplay. The book contains little in the way of moral judgements, allowing readers to learn freely from it and select and practise the parts they wish to.

The *Kama Sutra* also contains a lot of information about practices that are unacceptable today, such as how to charm lovers so you

4

could sleep with them without their knowledge, how to dispose of your lover's marriage partner, the correct rituals for being introduced to prostitutes and some quite dangerous and poisonous love potions.

The Ananga Ranga and the Khoka Shastra

Although the *Kama Sutra* is probably the best known of the Hindu erotic texts it is actually only one of a trilogy, the other two being the *Ananga Ranga* and the *Khoka Shastra*.

The *Khoka Shastra* was written by an Indian scholar, Khokkoka, in the twelfth century. It reflects how Indian society had changed in the eleven hundred years since the *Kama Sutra* and concentrates more on aspects of love rather than sexuality. It's more about sex within marriage and how to maintain and keep a long-term relationship sexually fresh and exciting.

The *Ananga Ranga* was written by Kalyaanamalla in the sixteenth century and was soon translated into Arabic where it became one of the most important Arabic sexual texts. It deals in detail with the sexual positions and updates the techniques of the earlier works.

By looking at the material available in all three volumes you can gain a considerable insight into Indian culture – such as more experimental lovemaking, enjoying sex in a long-term relationship, prolonging and enhancing foreplay, as well as an understanding of some of the Hindu sects such as the cult of Shiva and the symbolism of the phallic *lingam*.

Tantric Buddhism

We can also explore an exciting and different version of tantric sex – the sexual practices of the secret and little-known Buddhist sect which is dedicated to a union with God, through orgasm, by raising

kundalini energy. Tantric Buddhism is the much misunderstood practice of using the sexual energy as a way of exploring spirituality. It includes the techniques of prolonging intercourse, known as *karezza*, which can be easily learnt and practised. Some of the, until now, most secret techniques are revealed and explained so that we can incorporate them into our lovemaking and uniquely combine sex with spirituality – using sex as a gateway to a richer and deeper spiritual experience, and using spirituality as a means of expanding the sex act into one of erotic symbolism and meditation.

The techniques revealed have for centuries been shrouded in mystery. Here they are presented in a clear and easily understood way and include descriptions of the chakras or energy centres that are situated throughout the human body and the part they play in the kundalini energy's rise from the genitals to the higher spiritual centres in the brain.

The tantric Buddhists believe that we contain vast stores of dormant energy that lie sleeping in the area of our genitals, coiled like a serpent – the kundalini – and that, through sex, the energy can be woken, guided and used to increase our vitality, health and spiritual experience and, ultimately, that tantra, the Divine reunion, can be completed.

The tantric Buddhists picked up on the Hindu ideas, adapted them and refined them beyond most human's expectations. Few of us today would be prepared to devote quite so much time – the rest of our lives – to the pursuit of enlightenment through sex alone, yet there is much we can learn from the tantric Buddhists.

Tantrism in China

Around 750 AD Pu K'ung, a Chinese traveller, is reputed to have taken tantrism to China where he is regarded as the father of tantric Taoism (Taoism is the ancient religion of China). He learnt about tantra in Ceylon (now Sri Lanka). However Taoism predates even the *Kama Sutra* and the Chinese Taoists' knowledge of sexual matters was already highly developed before the concept of tantra

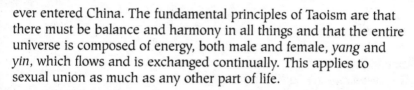

ever entered China. The fundamental principles of Taoism are that there must be balance and harmony in all things and that the entire universe is composed of energy, both male and female, *yang* and *yin*, which flows and is exchanged continually. This applies to sexual union as much as any other part of life.

The early Taoists wrote much on sexual matters and explored how the energy moves between partners. The Taoist approach is that sex is one of the basic forces of nature and shouldn't be repressed or denied but instead should be used to promote health, longevity and happiness. The longer each sexual union goes on the more energy is generated. The Taoists explored in great detail how to prolong sex so that the maximum benefit could be gained.

The Taoists produced 'pillow books' designed to help lovers enjoy sex, and as instructional manuals. The oldest of these is probably the sections of the *Huang-ti Nei Ching Su Wen* (the Yellow Emperor's classic of Internal Medicine) devoted to sex. It takes the form of a question and answer dialogue between Huang Ti, the Yellow Emperor, and one of his ministers, Ch'i Po, in which the Emperor asks questions and the minister gives answers on diet, lifestyle, moral codes, hygiene and ethics. His answers on sex are refreshingly open and liberated. He explains how the energy exchange that takes place between men and women during sex can be used to promote health and longevity. The Tao includes such interesting sexual positions as the 'Kicking Donkey', 'Lady Yin and the White Tiger' and 'Two Ducks Flying', and the sexual organs are unusually described as, for men: the 'Jade Stem' or the 'Heavenly Dragon', and, for women: the 'Vermilion Gate' or the 'Jade Pavilion'. So when the Heavenly Dragon enters the Jade Pavilion you can expect the 'Great Bursting of the Clouds'....

TANTRISM IN ARABIA

The Arabian empire had its own version of tantra – *The Perfumed Garden* – not only a delightful book of advanced sexual techniques but also a treatise on moral, social and dietary advice. This book

was written around 1600 AD; Sheikh Umar ibn Muhammed al-Nefzawi was commissioned by the Grand Vizier of Tunisia (then part of the Turkish Ottoman empire) to write a manual on the arts and techniques of love. Thus commanded, Nefzawi wrote *The Perfumed Garden*, and it is still one of the best-known erotic sex manuals in the world.

Nefzawi was a devout Muslim who saw sex as an example of God's sacred work and thus something to be enjoyed as a celebration of His gifts. Because of the Muslim disapproval of divorce, adultery being the third greatest sin of Islam after being an unbeliever or a murderer, *The Perfumed Garden* explores in some detail the role of sexuality in marriage and contains many useful and inventive techniques for stimulating and arousing your partner. This can help us keep the sexual excitement new and fresh during a long-term relationship. It also contains some wonderful descriptions of eleven classic positions, such as the 'Rainbow Arch' and the 'Pounding on the Spot', and six arousing movements such as the 'Seducer', the 'Race of the Member' and 'Love's Tailor' – with the advice to 'try each and all of them and settle for the ones which give both of you the greatest pleasure'.

Tantrism in Japan

Another area we will explore in some depth is the role eroticism plays in tantric sexuality. This is an area the Japanese have previously researched extensively and we can learn a great deal about our sexuality from their colourful and explicit *Shunga* or 'spring drawings'. These were given to young newly-weds on the first night of their honeymoon so that they could approach their first sexual experiences well prepared with visual aids. The drawings in the *Shunga* may be considered explicit by Western standards, perhaps even pornographic, as they invariably have enlarged or heavily emphasised genitalia. However, this was only partly titillation – they were mainly to be used as one would an instruction manual.

The lovers could laugh together over the drawings and if there was any embarrassment they could point to positions they wanted to try without having to discuss anything. The tradition of the *Shunga* only began to die out in the early part of the twentieth century, but in recent years they have been revived as people realised that young couples don't know everything – far from it when it comes to matters of sex.

The *Shunga* also feature erotic aids and oral sex in a very free and uninhibited way. The *Shunga* focuses heavily on the art of the erotic as a means of stimulating sexual passion and is derived from the ancient religion of Japan, Shinto, which says that sexual pleasure is the greatest of all – and therefore should be enjoyed as frequently as possible as well as in the most exciting way. The word 'Shinto' is of Chinese origin – the Japanese way of describing Shinto is *Kami no Michi*, which means the Way of the Gods, for the followers of Shinto see everything in nature as imbued with the spirits of the Gods. It's a very ancient religion and there is evidence that it was alive and active during the Stone Age. It has come down to us through the centuries with an organised priesthood and colourful ceremonies and rituals that reflect its basic joyous nature – there is little sense of sin – it's essentially a religion of gratitude and love.

Changing your focus

In *Tantric Sexuality* you will find the best of the techniques drawn from these ancient books so you can learn from other cultures, other periods of history, how to improve your lovemaking techniques as well as changing your sexual focus – from one of mere pleasure or procreation to one of a higher spiritual nature.

Tantric energy

Much of what you will learn in the following chapters concerns the movement of energy – *kundalini* to the Indians, *ch'i* to the Chinese – and it is necessary to have a thorough grounding in the philosophies

behind these concepts if you are to make real use of the techniques. We will explore the Taoist ideas of yin (female) and yang (male) energy and how we are all a unique blend of both, as well as the Indian concept of the chakras, energy centres situated throughout the body. You will learn how to explore this energy, how to begin to use it to raise your consciousness, how to channel it, and how to increase it – all through the enjoyable and exciting path of sexual awareness.

Who is this book for?

This book is written mainly for couples who are in a stable and loving relationship. Practising these techniques with someone who is not on the same 'wavelength' is not only pointless but could hinder your progress rather than help it. Although you will find some exercises that you can practise on your own, these are for learning about the energy and how your body functions rather than just being focused techniques.

Fundamental Differences

One of the fundamental differences between the Eastern and Western approach to sex is the concept of a goal or endproduct. In the West sex is seen as something that ends in orgasm, and without orgasm it is a disappointing or unrewarding experience. In the East sex is seen as a pleasurable journey; there may be no need of orgasm because the pleasure has been too intense already.

The other fundamental difference concerns male sexuality. In the West a male ejaculation is regarded as the same as his orgasm; while in the East a man's orgasm is something regarded as happening mostly without ejaculation. If the two happen simultaneously then that's a bonus. The idea of the male orgasm without ejaculation is something so alien to Western thinking that many men do not believe it to be possible. In this book men can learn the techniques that prove it not only to be possible, but they can learn how to do it for themselves.

Other aspects of tantric sexuality

We will also explore other important aspects of sexuality such as foreplay, oral sex, courtship, sex as meditation, erogenous zones, the right atmosphere for good sex, erotic kissing, sexual positions and sexual etiquette and health.

All of these topics are covered in the following chapters, but perhaps it's best if we begin by looking at exactly what the tantric practitioners mean by love and sex.

LOVE AND SEX

*Whoever offers me with devotion, a leaf, a flower, a fruit or water,
I accept that, the pious offering of the pure in heart. Whatever
you do, whatever you eat, whatever you offer in sacrifice,
whatever you give away, whatever path you follow, do it as an
offering to me.*

The Bhagavad Gita

DIVINE ENERGY

The tantric texts offer a wide and varied, sometimes conflicting,
body of advice concerning human sexuality; but the one area
they all agree on is the importance of sex within a loving and stable
relationship. To the tantric practitioners sex is not merely about a
simple act of pleasure but a deep and profound exchange of energy.
This energy is regarded as divine, a part of the energy of God or the
fundamental principle of the cosmos – whatever you want to call it:
spirit, soul, ch'i, kundalini, yogic life force. Thus when you are
having sex with someone you are taking part in both a physical
exchange of energy and a spiritual act of worship. By exchanging
energy you are acknowledging what that energy is, its importance
and its divinity. You aren't merely indulging in an act of procreation
but an act of ultimate love.

Shaking off your sexual inheritance

First though, before you can love another human being on such an intense and spiritual level you have to acknowledge the energy within yourself. Before loving another you have to be able to love yourself. As human beings we are bound up with guilt and embarrassment about our sexuality. This is part of our upbringing, especially if we have been brought up in the West. We are the inheritors of two thousand years of sexual bigotry and repression, and it isn't easy to shake that off quickly.

However shake it off we must if we are to take our true places as sexual beings who are capable of giving and receiving love on such an intimate and personal level. Before we can offer someone else the perfect gift of our bodies we have to be able to love our body as much as we expect our lover to love it. This is often a problem. Because of the nature of Western society we are brought up with a whole range of concepts about physical perfection. What woman hasn't despaired that she no longer looks as trim as the fashion models in the magazines? What man doesn't lament his hair loss or regret his expanding waistline? But our lovers are, on a very deep level, not seeking us out for our physical personae but as vessels of that divine energy – and as such we are perfect in their eyes. And if your body is getting larger then you might just be containing more of that energy to share with your partner!

Being comfortable with your body

For real tantric sex to happen you have to be both comfortable and happy with your body. It's no good wanting to be a sexually divine lover when you want to keep the lights off, hide under the covers and keep your clothes on – just because there's a few stretch marks

or some added poundage. Remember, your lover loves you as you are. It doesn't matter if you don't match up to some mythical image of beauty or thinness. Your lover cares only that you love each other and are together. If your lover is trying to change your physical self then you might be not quite on the same wavelength as each other.

EXERCISE 1

Although this exercise might at first glance appear silly or unimportant, what it reveals is the inner you and how you feel about yourself. When you're on your own find a full-length mirror and stand naked in front of it. Look objectively at yourself and listen to what goes on in your mind.

What you see is unimportant – it's only a container – but what you say to yourself is the revealing information. Are you OK about standing there in the nude? Do you feel free and liberated? Or guilty and shy? Only you can know what goes on in your head. But remember that this is what your lover sees when you make love – not your outer body, but a lover's heart sees all the stuff you carry around inside your head about your sexuality. That's what you've got to get rid off – all that stuff. And it's no good blaming anyone else: 'Oh, my mother made me feel this way about sex'; 'if it hadn't been for my first bad sexual encounter I'd be much more relaxed'; 'I've been hurt so many times I just can't trust any more'. When you stand naked in front of that mirror none of those people will be there.

Changing yourself

Only you are responsible for your sexuality and spiritual energy. Only you can change it. Even if you managed to get all the people responsible for the way you feel about sex together and you could accuse them, blame them and harangue them it wouldn't do you one iota of good – because only you can change what goes on inside your head. And the first change you can make is *acceptance*. What

you see is what you get – for better or worse – it's what you get and what your lover gets and loves. When you look at yourself be proud. What you see, believe it or not, is a perfect human being. You are exactly as your creator wanted you to be. How can you dare argue with your creator? If your creator can make mistakes, what hope have the rest of us got? According to the tantric practitioners what you see is a perfect representation of spiritual energy, that divinity in a human form. Isn't it fabulous?

The perfect you

Your human form is exactly as it was supposed to be – not too fat nor too thin, not too tall nor too short, not too old and not too young. Every line, every wrinkle, every blemish was put there to serve you, to improve you, to help you manifest in your glory. Be happy with what you see, be proud of the nakedness of the pure *you*. The world will not see your like again because there's only one of you, perfect and unique. Enjoy yourself.

Tantric sex is about appreciation

Tantric sex is about using sex to increase, improve, expand, explore and enjoy one's spirituality. It's not about casual encounters, group orgies, role playing, role models or even ego enhancement. Purely and simply it's about appreciation. Appreciating that the lover you are with is a container of divine energy and, as such, a perfect complement to your own energy. We will look in more detail in Chapter 4 at male and female energy, but for the moment you have to remember that you are a container of male or female energy and you need the balance of the opposite type.

Celibacy has no place in a book on tantric sex. No sex is as bad as unsatisfactory sex – and both of those are about the disharmony of

energy exchange. How many times have you had sex and felt worse afterwards? Recognising the importance of the energy exchanged, generated and enhanced is the first lesson of tantric sex.

EXERCISE 2

With your lover you can write down all your expectations of your partner. What do you want your lover to give you, do for you? What don't you like? What do you want to do that you've never dared ask or try? How do you want to be held? What sort of caresses do you like to give and receive?

When you have written down everything you can think of, give what you have written to your lover. What you will read will invariably, unless you're very connected, be a surprise. This exercise mustn't become the beginning of discord or argument. Instead you can learn a lot about your partner from it. Whatever your partner wants, expects, gives or receives is fine – and the same goes for you. In tantric sex there can be no right or wrong – only acceptance and recognition.

You have to do this exercise with two things in mind – honesty and no judgements. If you want to be in harmony with your partner you both have to be honest. And if your lover has been courageous enough to be honest then you have to accept it without judgement. A person's sexuality is a very vulnerable and delicate area – but there is no right or wrong. If your lover has certain reservations or what may appear to you to be strange notions or ideas then that is fine – because it's part of that person. Obviously the same goes for you – your feelings, ideas and wants are to be respected.

SEX AS A COMMUNICATION

When you read what your partner had written, did you know it already? If not what were you thinking of? The tantric texts were

written as a means of communication. Enhancing sex is the same – *communication*. This communication between lovers can be spoken or not – just so long as it takes place. We all need to be cared about, to be comforted, to be loved, to be caressed and worshipped – but how many of us know how to ask for these things? Or indeed that it is our right to expect them? But first we have to be prepared to give them. We cannot give unless we know what is wanted of us, what is expected. To know that, we have to be prepared to listen, to be aware of our partner's needs. We cannot be open to another's needs if we are consumed with our own. To give wholeheartedly, without reservation, without expectation of reward or reciprocal gifts is the first and hardest lesson of tantric sex.

When we are aware that our partner's needs are ultimately important we can give ultimately to our partner. And thus it will be given back to us unconditionally. We cannot expect this return of love – it's a bonus when it happens. But we have to be the ones to make the first declaration of unconditional worship, that's the way it works. We give first and then are rewarded – sometimes. But we always give first.

Taking and receiving

Western sex is about taking first, tantric sex is about giving first. We must give away some of ourselves before there's any space to receive something of somebody else. And we need that something if we are to be truly realised, well-rounded and complete human beings.

If your partner is not truly and totally sexually satisfied how can you expect your partner to be harmonious enough to please you? This works for both of you by the way. Neither one of you can say 'you have to give to me first'. We both must be ready to give to each other at the same time. Giving can be one of the most rewarding of all activities, not something we are used to in the West where the 'me first' attitude has deprived us all of a richer experience. Giving to our lover also means we must make time for that person.

EXERCISE 3

You can try this exercise on alternate days or nights. The beauty of this exercise is that there is no going first. Whoever gives first receives also. Let's suppose it's the woman who is to receive first. Her partner should run her a warm bath and prepare the bathroom with incense and candles. Make an occasion of it. She can relax and enjoy the bath while her lover washes her all over. She must tell him how she likes her hair washed, let him do it for her. She is being worshipped as a representation of the ultimate female energy.

After her bath she should find somewhere warm to lie down – perhaps on a rug in front of the fire. Her lover can then massage her with essential oils. This is not a therapeutic massage to ease muscular aches and tension (although it may well do that as a bonus) but rather a massage so her lover can explore her body, caress her in a non-sexual way. He should touch and soothe every part of her body until she feels her skin shine and burst with energy. She must tell him how she feels, which bits feel best, where she likes being touched most, how much pressure to use, how his hands feel on her body. This massage usually produces a warm soporific effect but can also induce sexual tension as well.

Her lover should bring her to orgasm if she likes by using his fingers, tongue and mouth. But this exercise is not about having sex, it's caressing, exploring and touching. Let him do all the touching. If she wants him naked as well that's fine, but it's a massage for her. She doesn't have to attend to his sexual needs in any way. This is his opportunity to worship the female divinity in her – the Shakti or Goddess. Enjoy the feeling of not only being worshipped but also being the Goddess herself in human form – for that's what she is and as such is entitled to be worshipped.

The next day it's the man's turn to be worshipped. Again he should let his partner bathe and wash him. And let her give him the same soothing massage. Tell her which bits he likes touched, where he feels warmth and caresses from her hands. He is being worshipped as the representation, in human form, of the God

Shiva, for that's what he is. If he wishes, he can let his partner bring him to orgasm using her hands and mouth but remember, and this is important for men, real sex is not about orgasm.

No orgasm? But...

Tantric sex is about the energy generated by and during sex – and that is something separate from the male orgasm. In the West we are very goal oriented. We believe that every sexual encounter must end in orgasm or we will not be satisfied or fulfilled. However this is simply not true. There are many practitioners of tantric sex who have refrained for years from ejaculating (which in the West we equate with orgasm) without losing anything from their sex lives; rather they have gained immeasurably.

Once we lose the need to be so focused on our orgasm we can begin to enjoy the journey. However, since you are just starting out you can still have your orgasm for this exercise, but it might be beneficial to try it again on another occasion and to deliberately decide not to

have an orgasm and see how it feels. We will look at enhancing the male orgasm in Chapter 6. You may find the exercise feels more satisfying because it has no end, no conclusion. If it ends in orgasm, there is then a need to find another focus, to move on to something else. But if it doesn't end in orgasm then the feeling of being worshipped as Shiva continues, and the afterglow remains.

Loving relationships

So how necessary to tantric sex is a loving relationship? Well, the tantrics would say that if lovers don't have time to learn about each other they cannot know each other. If you don't know your lover's sexual preferences and needs, you can't be a good lover. The idea of a 'one-night stand' to the tantrics would be quite abhorrent. How can you learn everything you need to know in one night? And if you're not learning about your partner's needs what are you doing? Surely then you must be going for purely selfish sexual gratification? If that's the case then the energy will be all wrong. You can't share energy if you're thinking only of your own needs. Perhaps the ancient tantrics also had a little foresight; the need for a stable relationship becomes increasingly important in this day of sexually transmitted diseases and potentially fatal viruses.

Energy trails

The whole idea of energy exchange during sexual activity is fairly new to the West; however, in the East it has long been recognised. And that energy exchange is on a permanent basis. You carry with you all the energy trails of all your past lovers. If your sexual encounters are brief and hurried, or shameful and negative, then that's the sort of energy you will be carrying and passing on to your next lover who, in turn, will inherit that energy. The cycle must stop somewhere. In the next few chapters you can learn how to purify or alter that energy; turning it from cold and negative into warm and loving – something you'd be proud to share with another person.

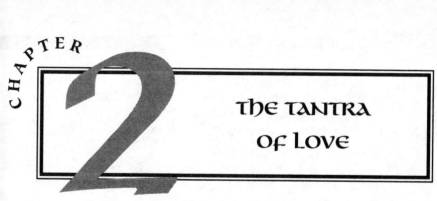

THE TANTRA
OF LOVE

Kindle the fire of love and burn away all things, then set thy foot into the land of the lovers.

Baha'u'llah

THE POWER OF LOVE

Most of the tantric texts agree that love is one of the most fundamental and energetic forces a human being can encounter. That force can be used positively to progress one's spiritual experience. They say that the love we can feel for another human being is but a tiny part of the love we can feel for God and that sex is a physical manifestation of that love. They feel that sex when enjoyed with the right focus is a powerful tool, and one that can be used with God's blessing.

It may seem strange to Westerners that sex can be enjoyed freely and yet still be part of a spiritual or religious life. This approach is somewhat different from Western religions where sex is often seen as something to be repressed or denied.

THE CHAKRAS

The tantric texts agree that there is a movement of energy within the human body during sex that can be both felt and used. This energy

is physical. It rises up during the arousal of sex and can be directed and channelled. According to the Hindu tantric texts we have within us six energy centres known as chakras. These energy centres each have a specific area of human life that they are said to control.

- The base chakra – *Muladhara* – is situated at the base of the spine between the genitals and the anus. This chakra governs our instincts and genetic coding. It is usually represented by a yellow square. The mantra for the base chakra is *lam*.

- The pelvic chakra – *Swadhishthana* – is situated at the genitals themselves. This chakra governs our sexual life. It is usually represented by a white crescent. The mantra for the pelvis chakra is *vam*.

- The navel chakra – *Manipuraka* – is situated at the navel. This chakra governs our personal power. It is usually represented by a red triangle. The mantra for the navel chakra is *ram*.

- The heart chakra – *Anahata* – is situated at the heart. This chakra governs our love. It is usually represented by a blue hexagon. The mantra for the heart chakra is *yam*.

- The throat chakra – *Vishuddha* – is situated at the throat. This chakra governs our communication. It is usually represented by a white circle. The mantra for the throat chakra is *ham*.

- The brow chakra – *Ajna* – is situated between the brows. This chakra governs our intellect and thought processes. It is usually represented by an inverted white triangle. The mantra for the brow chakra is *om*.

Each of these chakras also has a Hindu god attributed to it as well as various symbolic animals, flowers, elements, seasons and a letter of the Sanskrit alphabet. For a more detailed study of the chakras, see *Chakras for Beginners* in this series. We need only be concerned with the basics in this book.

tbe crown chakra

There is also another chakra worth considering; this is not a true chakra like the others but rather is known as a *shuddha* and it is situated at the crown of the head. It is sometimes known as the crown chakra but it doesn't operate in quite the same way as the others. Its name is *sahasrara* and it is the home of the Goddess Shakti – the God Shiva is said to reside in the brow chakra. The whole point of raising the kundalini energy from the base chakra up the spine to the brow chakra, and then on the crown chakra, is to free Shiva so he may be reunited with Shakti, and the great cosmic reunion of the male and female principles can take place. This state of divine bliss is known as *samadhi* – enlightenment.

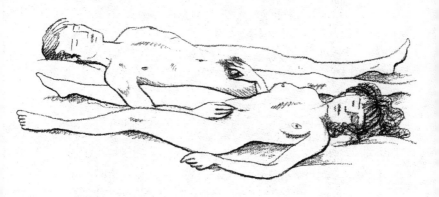

Tantric Yoga Relaxation Position

EXERCISE 1

FOR THE MAN

You should lie down somewhere warm and comfortable. Imagine the site of each chakra as a small tightly furled flower or small leather bag. As you breathe out make the mantra sound for each chakra as you visualise it in turn, starting with the base chakra and finishing with the brow chakra. Imagine each chakra to be a flower opening as you breathe out – or the small leather bag having draw strings which are being slowly loosened.

Work your way up your body imagining each chakra opening as you make the mantra sound as you exhale. You need to do this exercise with your eyes closed so you can visualise each chakra in turn. This exercise can be done before you make love with your partner so that you are fully open and ready to feel energy moving within your body.

FOR THE WOMAN

You should lie down somewhere warm and comfortable. Imagine each chakra as a flower turned upside down. As you breathe out make the sound of the chakra mantra and imagine each chakra in turn, starting with the base chakra and finishing with the crown chakra, to be the flower slowly turning until it is upright. As it does so, imagine it becoming cooler and stiller as if filled with cold refreshing energy.

You should do this exercise before making love with your partner so that your chakras are open and you are ready to feel the energy moving within your body.

PURIFYING ENERGY

You can both also do this exercise as a method of cleansing or purifying your energy. As you visualise your energy reaching the crown chakra imagine it pouring out of the top of your head and being replaced with fresh new energy from your base chakra. Imagine all the collected energy of all your past lovers being replaced so that you can begin again with a fresh supply.

EXERCISE 2

TANTRIC YOGA RELAXATION POSITION (MULADHARA SADHANA)

Both you and your lover lie down side by side on your backs but facing opposite ways – your feet to your lover's head and vice versa. The man should lie with the woman along his right side so he can place his right hand lightly across her vulva. The woman can then use her right hand to hold his penis lightly.

This is an exercise to feel the energy rising from the base chakra up through the pelvic chakra and beyond. Try to feel the warmth your lover's hand generates in and through your genitals. As the warmth spreads, focus on it and feel it spreading upwards as energy.

The man will feel this energy slowly working its way up his spine, whilst for the woman the energy will rise slowly up through her belly first and then her breasts. The man's energy, being hotter and more volatile, may well rise faster but he should not rush it. The woman's energy, being cooler and slower to arouse, will take longer. If during this exercise either becomes aroused to the point of orgasm then that's all right. Because we are orgasm-oriented in the West it may take a while to learn to focus on the energy rather than the sexual/spiritual experience. Whatever way you do it, it should be an enjoyable experience. The whole basis of raising the kundalini energy is to share and experience the 'godhead' – if this isn't done in a spirit of delight and enjoyment it will not be successful. There are some who have spent a whole lifetime practising tantric sex and getting nowhere because they do the whole thing as a ritual and miss the point completely.

AROUSAL AND ENJOYMENT

You have to enter into tantric sex with an approach of delight – what happens is happening and it's all right. Sometimes there will be a union of soul with soul and sometimes not – but the journey

should be enjoyed without thought of the destination, or the experience that is presented along the way will be lost.

If, during Exercise 2, you become aroused, enjoy it. And there should be no spiritual ego to taunt your partner with: 'Oh, I attained enlightenment and all you achieved was orgasm'.

Using kundalini energy

Use the experience as it comes and try to use the energy in a beneficial way. The principal aim or objective of raising the kundalini energy is to reunite or connect with the energy of the universe through the unique and wonderful experience of sex. Tantra is a reunion with God.

The three forms of energy

During Exercise 3 the energy may become very sleepy – go with it and use the time given as a meditation. Focus on the brow chakra (see page 22) and allow yourself to appreciate what you can see, feel and hear. There is a reason, according to the tantric Buddhists, why the energy can take any one of many different forms. It may be orgasmic, meditative or spiritually enlightening – it may even be all three – but the energy generated is being transformed into exactly what you need at any given moment. It may not be what you expect or even what you particularly want, but it will be what you need. The tantric Buddhists recommend that you go with it; if you don't fight the universe it will provide you with everything you need.

Being in touch with your body

Exercise 3 will put you in touch with your genital feelings. We focus on our genitals usually only in the rush of orgasm or if they are being

caressed. During this exercise you can focus on both yours and your partner's genitals. How do they feel? Wholesome and healthy? Or is there some residue guilt or inhibition there? According to the tantric Buddhists one of the reasons we sometimes fail to achieve a truly deep spiritual/sexual experience is because we are somehow hanging on to our fears and repression. During Exercise 3 you can explore your feelings about your sexuality – and your body as a sexual instrument.

EXERCISE 3

CHAKRA SEX POSITION

The man should sit on the floor and the woman should straddle him. He should insert his erect penis into her vulva, but neither should move. If the woman grasps the man around his back and he holds her around her shoulders, both should be able to relax and feel comfortable. Look into each other's eyes. The tantric texts suggest that you should both keep your tongue on the roof of your mouth as this helps the energy complete its circuit around your body.

You should both feel the warmth coming from each other's pelvic chakra and concentrate on feeling the energy rising up.

The woman should feel the energy as a cool flow rising slowly up the front of her body. The man should feel the energy as a hot flow rising up his spine. This position is more about meditation than sex, although you may both orgasm in this position without moving. It gives you both a chance to relax and feel or visualise the energy moving without any expectations. It's also very good for lovers who have problems with the man experiencing premature ejaculation. As there is no movement, no thrusting excitement, he should be able to keep his penis in position for quite a while before experiencing ejaculation. Again there are no expectations. If you don't feel any energy moving you can visualise it instead. If only one of you feels the energy, then that's also fine.

Sometimes this position is very good prior to making love as a means of establishing a contact, a sort of spiritual reaffirmation of your love for each other. How long you spend in this position

is entirely up to you. It's something you need to find out by experimentation. For some couples a few minutes seem to be enough, while other couples will enjoy this position so much that they are content to spend a considerable amount of time doing it.

If you do tire you can always lean back for a while and rest. You may even like to experiment by eating or drinking while doing this. You can talk to each other, tell each other stories. This position is about relaxing with each other, feeling the energy, and trust. You don't have to do anything, go anywhere. Just be together in the most intimate way without wanting the other to be anything or anyone else – just be yourselves.

You can always try experimenting if you find this position uncomfortable. The man can sit in a chair, one without arms like a wooden kitchen chair, and the woman can sit astride him. He can then support her with his hands on her hips and she can rest her arms on his shoulders or even grip the back of the chair.

Chakra Sex Position

EXERCISE 4

This is an exercise for you to do either alone or together. Doing it alone is somewhat easier but it's up to you. If you try it alone first you should bring yourself to orgasm in the way that suits you best. Masturbation is highly recommended by the tantric texts as a means of getting in touch with your own sexuality; of finding out how things work and learning about the energy flow.

As you reach orgasm you should concentrate on the energy flow. Feel energy instead of simply experiencing the pleasure.

For the man you can imagine that you have a pump at the base of the spine and it's going to pump the energy up your spine. As you orgasm you can clench and unclench your buttocks; imagine this is the pump doing all the work.

For the woman you can imagine that the pump is located in your vaginal muscles. As you orgasm, squeeze your vaginal muscles in repeated contractions and relaxations so that you get the effect of a pump. Imagine the energy being pumped up the front of your body.

Safety and confidence

You can experiment with these exercises in complete safety. You might like to do Exercise 1 of this chapter before doing Exercise 4 so that your chakras are open and the energy has a good pathway to flow up. You may hear people suggest that experimenting with kundalini energy is dangerous or forbidden – well, it's safe and it's yours. You can do anything you like with it, experiment as much as you like, try what you will and find out how you feel about it all. If you feel uncomfortable with any of it you can stop. If, however, it makes you feel good or improves your sex life then you can continue with it. If you like it do it, if you don't then don't do it. It really is that simple. There is no danger and there are no rules.

Exploring your body

Please feel free to explore and learn as much about your own body and your lover's as you wish. The only requirement is to remember that this is tantric sex – sex with a focus on spirituality. However, even that will be forgotten sometimes when passion will overtake you, and that's fine as well. Sex is not a serious business; it's designed to be enjoyed and appreciated. If there are times you want to laugh or have fun instead of doing it all seriously then that's a good thing.

If you want to try Exercise 4 together you should take it in turns to stimulate the other to orgasm, then relax and feel the energy. You can, of course, even masturbate each other at the same time but it can then be quite hard to concentrate as you would have three things to be focused on: your own orgasm, your partner's and your own energy rising – that's not to say you can't, only that it takes a lot of effort and if you have little success it may not be the energy failing to rise but you failing to detect it because you're distracted by having to concentrate on your partner's orgasm. The energy is quite subtle and if you are unused to feeling it, it can be easy to miss or fail to notice. After a few attempts you may feel the energy much more strongly and then you can incorporate other methods of loving into your repertoire.

Back To back

One suggested method of doing Exercise 4 is for you both to sit back to back. Bring yourself to orgasm and experience the energy as you pump. You may even feel your partner's energy rising as your backs are in such close contact. If you feel nothing it doesn't matter as this variation on the exercise is fun and may be something you haven't tried before.

In Chapter 3 we will look at how we can exchange sexual energy with our partners.

3

BEGINNING TANTRIC SEX

It is not only that a man could nurture his Yang by taking Yin essence from the woman. A woman could also take Yang essence from the man to nurture her.

Chung Ho Tzu, sixth-century Chinese Taoist

Exchanging energy

It may seem a strange notion to Westerners – that we can physically exchange energy during sex. However, there are some practical exercises you can do which may convince you of the reality of such an experience as well as allowing you to experiment freely with your own energy and that of your partner.

The Hindu tantric practitioners write about the energy as the *kundalini* – the coiled serpent – while the Chinese Taoists describe it as *ch'i* which we will look at in Chapter 4.

Using your tongue

If you have practised some of the exercises in Chapter 2 you may now have an understanding of the kundalini energy. In one of the exercises the advice was to keep your tongue touching the roof of your mouth. This is to allow the energy to freely complete its circuit around the body. By using your tongue like this you can feel the

energy as it flows. The Chinese believe the tongue to be an internal organ – the only one we can see and experience externally. It is a very sensitive instrument and can channel and control the energy in a very delicate way. During our lovemaking we instinctively lick and suck parts of our lover's body. As well as producing exquisite pleasure in them it is also an instinctive attempt to experience that energy – and it can be done so much more effectively if we do it consciously.

KISSING

One of the ways we can truly experience our energy consciously is when we are kissing. The art of kissing is a skill that takes time to learn and lots of practice if we are to experience it fully. And it's an art not often practised in the West. In China couples won't kiss in public as they regard it as something so intimate, so sexual, that it would be like making love in public.

EXERCISE 1

EROTIC KISSING

Agree with your partner to spend as much time practising erotic kissing as you can. You can use your lips and tongue to explore your partner's mouth. You can suck the tongue, lick the inside of the lips, nip with your teeth, even exchange saliva – known as the 'juice of jade' in China. You can use your tongue to explore your lover's entire face: lick the eyelids, ears and the underside of the chin (this is particularly erotic). If you and your partner suck each other's tongue in turn you may find it quite easy to orgasm spontaneously.

Another aspect of erotic kissing is to use your fingers as well. As you lick and suck on your partner's mouth you can both insert your fingers into each other's mouth and suck on the fingers as

well. Obviously in all of these exercises some degree of personal hygiene is important. Clean your teeth beforehand and avoid strong tasting or smelling foods.

You can use your tongue to explore your partner's hands. The skin between the fingers is especially sensitive. Most men report that having their thumbs sucked is very erotic both because of its resemblance to oral sex but also because of the sensitivity of the thumb.

EXERCISE 2

EXPLORING SKIN

You can use your tongue to explore the entire skin area of your partner's body. To completely lick every part of another's body takes longer than you might think – but it's worth it. Lovers get to know each other pretty intimately as well as finding out exactly what turns them on, which bits they like licked the best. It's quite common to expect the erogenous zones to be sensitive but you may be surprised to find that the crook of the elbow produces such a strong reaction, or the armpit, or the bottom of the feet, or the back of the knees.

Nipples are very sensitive as are navels, throats, foreheads and genitals – these are the areas of the chakras. It's not just that these areas are sensitive because they're sexy – it's also because they are major energy centres.

While doing this exercise lovers should be concentrating both on giving each other pleasure and also on feeling what their energy is doing. If you take your time you may well begin to feel tiny electric currents in your tongue as you reach the right spot on your lover's body where the energy is being generated as well.

You could also try visualising energy as tiny sparks jumping from the tip of your tongue. If you do this you may find your partner reacts differently – as if there really are sparks flying.

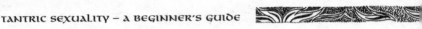
EXERCISE 3

USING YOUR TONGUE

After a time spent erotically kissing and exploring all of the skin of each other's body you may like to bring your lover to orgasm using your tongue and lips only. Again concentrate on the energy being generated. As you lick and suck you can try visualising that energy – again see it as tiny sparks jumping from the end of your tongue. If you keep your eyes closed try to concentrate on the area between your eyebrows and in the centre of your forehead – the 'third eye'. Watch what happens there as you reach orgasm yourself. Instead of seeing darkness you may be surprised by how much light is generated by the energy of the kundalini reaching the top of your head. This is energy you can see as well as feel.

When you are bringing your partner to orgasm feel what happens to the tip of your tongue – can you feel the energy? When you are reaching your own orgasm, keep your tongue on the roof of your mouth and feel what happens.

EXERCISE 4

MORE EROTIC KISSING

Bring your partner to orgasm using your hands. As orgasm is reached suck your partner's tongue quite hard and practise the erotic kissing techniques. Your partner should now bring you to orgasm and you can try the same thing – feel what happens to your tongue when it is sucked hard as you reach orgasm.

After orgasm you should always practise erotic kissing together – it promotes intimacy as well as being an extremely sensitive way of keeping the energy flowing. If you don't subside too far after orgasm it's easier to continue.

EXERCISE 5

SOUL BARING

Let your partner bring him or herself to orgasm while you practise erotic kissing. Use your fingers to explore your partner's mouth as well as your lips and tongue. As orgasm is reached hold your partner's face in your hands and look deeply into the eyes and watch what happens there. Then it's your turn. Keep your eyes open as you reach orgasm and look into your partner's eyes.

This exercise requires a considerable degree of intimacy, love and trust. This is one of those exercises you couldn't do with a casual sexual partner – there's too much soul baring. And you are doing exactly that, baring your soul to your partner and allowing access to the most intimate, inner part of you. It certainly requires trust, but if you try it you may find it an incredible experience – one that you will want to repeat often. It raises sex from being a merely physical pleasure to being one of such intensity and spirituality that you wonder why you haven't been doing it for years.

EXERCISE 6

USING THE CHAKRAS

We are used to bringing our partners to orgasm by concentrating our energies on their pelvic chakra, but what about trying the other chakras? The nipples are in the region of the heart chakra. Try bringing your partner to orgasm by sucking, licking, feeling, pinching, tweaking the nipples – and they can try doing the same to you.

Try bringing each other to orgasm by concentrating your loving on your throat chakras, or brow chakras, or navel chakras. And don't forget the base chakra. You will find this midway between the

genitals and the anus. It's called the perineum and it is extremely sensitive. You can try bringing your partner to orgasm by licking this area or massaging it with your fingers. A woman can get her partner to insert his fingers into her anus and vagina and grip the perineum, massaging it internally. A man can get his partner to massage the area underneath his testicles and insert her finger into his rectum. Obviously these techniques require hygiene – if you insert a finger into your partner's anus you should wash your hands before using your fingers anywhere else. And if your partner has any reservations about such techniques then those reservations should be respected, as should yours.

EXERCISE 7

FOLLOWING THE PATH

Using your tongue follow the path the kundalini energy would follow in your partner's body. For the man this is up the spine. The woman can start with her tongue on his perineum and trace the passage of the energy over his buttocks and over his spine to the top of his head. She can continue down his brow, throat, chest and back to the perineum. The man can masturbate while the woman is doing this and they can feel the energy rising in different ways. The man can visualise the energy as it goes up through the chakras.

For the woman the energy rises the opposite way so the man should trace the energy flow up the front of her body. He should start with his tongue on his partner's perineum and trace the path from her vulva, up across her belly, between her breasts, up her throat to her brow and then stop at the crown of her head. If she masturbates while he does this, aim to time orgasm to happen as the man's tongue reaches the crown of her head. As the orgasm subsides the man should run his tongue down her spine and back to her perineum.

Following the path

EXERCISE 8

DIFFERENT TEMPERATURES

You can try experimenting with different temperatures on your tongue. Keep some ice cubes handy as well as a hot drink. Dip your tongue into these alternately and see what effect it has on your partner. Try practising oral sex using an ice cube or hot drink held in the mouth so your partner gets the full effect of the heightened temperature. As the orgasm happens you can try suddenly switching the temperature and see what happens. Try running ice cubes over your partner's nipples or genitals. Try whatever you both fancy. You can only learn about the energy by experimenting. And you can only experiment by having fun.

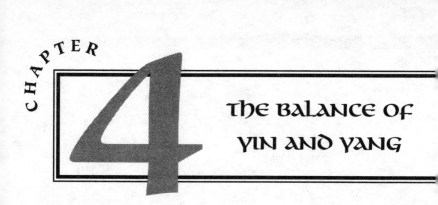

THE BALANCE OF YIN AND YANG

Women, being of tender nature, want tender beginnings, and when they are forcibly approached by men with whom they are but slightly acquainted, they sometimes suddenly become haters of sexual connection, and sometimes even haters of the male sex.

The *Kama Sutra*

Heaven as a circle

The ancient religion of China is Taoism. The Taoists believe that in the beginning there was Heaven represented by a circle. From heaven there was created Matter (earth) represented by a square. The circle became an unbroken line (yang), and the square became a broken line (yin). Yang was heaven, the sky, light, the male principle and yin was matter, the earth, dark, the female principle.

The yin broken line and the yang unbroken line could be used together in various combinations to give compass directions, the elements, the *I Ching* (Book of Changes) and that most famous of all symbols, the yin/yang.

The Taoists believe that all humans are made of a unique blend of yin and yang, but women are predominantly yin while men are mostly yang. But like the yin/yang symbol we contain within us the seed of the other – we cannot be one alone. The Taoists, from experience, attributed various qualities to both yin and yang. These qualities don't require you to believe in Taoism: they can be demonstrated by experiment and experience. These qualities are:

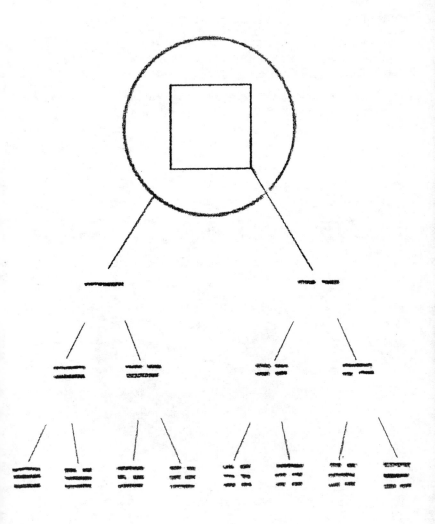

The circle and square, and the I Ching symbols

- **Yin** – shadow, wet, soft, cold, night, dark, receptive, female, passive, negative, inner, emotional, deep, interior, winter, absorbing, retiring, nurturing, proactive.

- **Yang** – sun, dry, hard, warm, day, light, creative, male, active, positive, outer, intellectual, shallow, surface, summer, repelling, advancing, aggressive, reactive.

It certainly doesn't mean that all women will demonstrate all the yin qualities nor a man all the yang ones. But there will be a predominance of them in each of us.

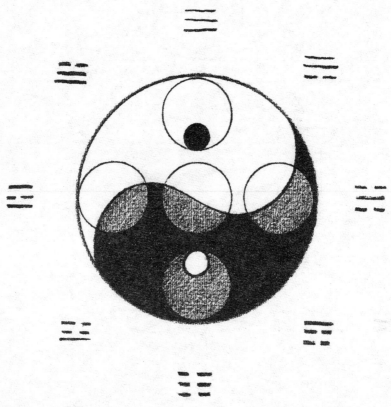

The yin/yang with elements

ThE ELEMENTS

It's also useful to look at the way the Taoists regard elements. There are five – fire, water, wood, metal, and earth. Earth is usually seen as being in the centre with the other four arranged around the outside.

You will notice that two of these elements come under the auspices of yin – metal and water, and two under yang – fire and wood. Metal is known as the 'lesser yin'; water as the 'greater yin'. Wood is the 'lesser yang'; fire the 'greater yang'. Metal is known as the 'face of beauty', water as the 'giver of life'. Wood and fire are known as the 'eyes and ears of the universe' respectively.

Their attributes are:

- **Earth** – *T'u* – the diplomat, moderate with a sense of loyalty. A harmonious person who likes to belong. Earth types pay attention to and like detail. They like company and like to be liked. They can be stubborn. They help metal and are helped by fire. They hinder water and are hindered by wood.

- **Fire** – *Huo* – the magician, compassionate and intuitive. Fire types like to communicate and they love pleasure. They seek excitement and like to be in love. They don't like to be bored. They help earth and are helped by wood. They hinder metal and are hindered by water.

- **Water** – *Shui* – the philosopher, imaginative and honest, clever and original. Water types seek knowledge and are tough and independent. They can be secretive and they like to be protected. They help wood and are helped by metal. They hinder fire and are hindered by earth.

- **Metal** – *Chin* – the catalyst, organised, precise and controlling. Metal types are discriminating but they do like to be right. They like order and cleanliness. They appreciate quality. They help water and are helped by earth. They hinder wood and are hindered by fire.

- **Wood** – *Mu* – the pioneer, expansive and purposeful. Wood types are active and like to be busy. They can be domineering and they desperately need to win. They are very practical. They help fire and are helped by water. They hinder earth and are hindered by metal.

So which are you? Which do you want to be? What element is your lover? Have you just learnt something about each other you didn't know?

How can you tell which type you are?

All you have to do is look up the year you were born in the chart below.

Year ending	Element	Attribute
0	metal	yang
1	metal	yin
2	water	yang
3	water	yin
4	wood	yang
5	wood	yin
6	fire	yang
7	fire	yin
8	earth	yang
9	earth	yin

Let's suppose you were born in a year ending in a 3 – say 1963. That would make you the element yin water. You would display the characteristics of water – the philosopher – in a yin fashion: you would flow like water but in a deep darker way. You might be the philosopher but in a very imaginative and honest fashion. Your ideal partner might be yang wood.

The Chinese calendar

There are many different ways of working out which element you may be. I have given you a well-used and reliable Chinese system

but there are others. You will also have to watch out for the first months of each year as the Chinese calendar is different from ours, and the months at the beginning of the year vary from year to year. But this is an example of the sort of information you can glean from knowing which element you are and what your partner is.

And once we know what element our partner is we can alter or change our lovemaking techniques to help and improve our lovemaking. You wouldn't approach a yang fire type in quite the same way as you'd approach a yin water type.

Yin energy—yang energy

You don't always need to work with elements but you do need to have an understanding of the way yin energy and yang energy work. If you look at the list of attributes for each fundamental principle you will notice that yin energy is darker, cooler, deeper, whereas yang energy is lighter, hotter, closer to the surface. And likewise men (yang) are often quicker to arouse; their energy is hot and rapid, immediate and brief. Women (yin) are slower to arouse, more sustained, taking longer to peak and longer to cool down afterwards. Men, with their quick hot energy should appreciate that their lover might take longer to reach orgasm, need more caressing and attention, appreciate more intimacy and loving afterwards and be capable of more sustained sexual activity. They may be much more inclined to generate the right atmosphere and conditions for lovemaking. Men, on the other hand, are much more quickly aroused, especially by visual images, and much less needful of long prolonged foreplay. They are also less concerned with atmosphere. Some of these qualities you may recognise and others you may not. There is nothing sexist in Taoist philosophy but only observations based on thousands of years of study.

EXERCISE 1

A good way to find out more about the differences in energy is to do this exercise. Again you will need to take it in turn.

YANG ENERGY

Let's say it's the man's turn to go first. He should lie down somewhere warm and comfortable. The woman will give him a yang massage. She should start by holding his penis and with her other hand begin a series of short gentle circular stroking movements from his genital region outwards. All the while she should hold his penis in one hand and massage with the other. The massage should end with his face. Then the woman can bring him to orgasm using her hands, lips, and mouth. The man can then choose to do exactly what he wants. He may choose to sleep – there must be no judgement in this: this is his time and anything is fine.

YIN ENERGY

When it's the woman's turn she, too, should lie down somewhere warm and comfortable and the man will give her a yin massage. He should start by caressing her face with both hands. One hand should stay in contact with her face at all times and the other hand can massage her in a long, gentle spiral with her vulva as the centre. This should be the last area he massages and he can then bring her to orgasm using hands, lips and mouth. She can then chose what she wants to do – to be held or caressed, or to go to sleep.

IS THE ENERGY DIFFERENT?

Afterwards you can both talk about what you have felt and how it felt for the masseur or masseuse. Does the energy feel different? Are men quicker to arouse? Do they need less foreplay? Are women slower to arouse but capable of longer, deeper and more intense orgasms?

If you are both aware that there may be differences in energy levels and intensity you may become more considerate lovers; more ready to provide each other with what you need if you appreciate that your needs are different, and come from a very deep place – one of an instinctive energy fulfilment.

ENERGY CYCLES

It's also interesting to look at the cycles of energy we experience. The Taoists believed that women's energy flowed over a monthly cycle, whereas a man's peaked on a daily basis – about eighteen times a day. This gives him a complete change round in mood about every hour and a half. Women tend to be, according to the Taoists, more emotionally stable because they have a longer cycle. Is this your experience?

CHING

The other fundamental difference between Taoist belief and Western sexual practices is the notion of *ching*. Ching is often translated as 'sperm', but it isn't. Ching is the energy released in the sperm during ejaculation. The Taoists believed that a man could orgasm without ejaculating, that the orgasm is a separate thing entirely. If a man ejaculated too often he would lose valuable ching and thus his energy levels would drop too much. The Taoists believed longevity and ching levels were connected. Too little ching leads to ill health, whereas lots of ching could enable a man to live long and healthily. We will deal with this more thoroughly in the next couple of chapters.

5

THE EASTERN
APPROACH TO
ORGASM

Those who know the Tao of Loving and harmonise the yin and yang are able to blend the five joys into a heavenly pleasure; those who do not know the Tao of Loving will die before their time, without even really having enjoyed the pleasure of loving.

Su Nu Ching

SEX IS A JOURNEY

M ost of the tantric texts agree that sex is a journey. There is no destination. An orgasm may be a stopping-off point, a sort of station along the way, but it is not the end of the line. In the West the orgasm does tend to be the end of the sexual act. Couples have their orgasm, either together or individually, and that's it – the sex is over for another day, or night.

The summit of the mountain

In the East sex is seen as something which couples do over a much longer period of time – it may last for hours. An orgasm may be seen almost as a distraction under these circumstances. Or the orgasm may be seen as a relief in a long journey. The aim is to keep taking the sensations higher and higher – why stop at the lowlands when you can reach the summit of the mountain?

Why we need orgasms

We looked at ch'i energy in Chapter 4 and the Taoists belief that yin or female energy is much deeper and cooler than the yang or male energy. It is richer and darker and it feeds the yang energy with life. The Taoists recommend that the male orgasm is kept to a minimum – especially ejaculatory orgasm, and we will see why and how in Chapter 7. They also recommend that women can have more orgasms than men because their energy levels are capable of sustaining a higher level of orgasm. The Taoists also believe that women need to discharge this yin energy before it builds up into too great an amount which can lead to ill health, depression and nervous disorders. Her orgasms keep her fresh and young and feed her partner with energy that he can then use to go on giving her more orgasms. We will look at how the female orgasm works and how to improve it in Chapter 6. But for the moment it's worth pondering on the truth of Taoist belief. Obviously, for all men and women physical reactions and responses will be different. But what is your experience? Does what the Taoists say make sense? As an exercise over the next few lovemaking sessions you could concentrate on those yin and yang energy levels and see if there isn't some truth in what the Taoists say.

The orgasm as a spiritual experience

Some tantric texts, especially the Hindu ones, recommend the orgasm as a spiritual experience and say that it should be approached and enjoyed as a religious practice only. Maybe the two systems are not that incompatible. If the orgasm is treated as lightly as it is in the West it becomes devalued. Both the Hindus and the Taoists are suggesting that the orgasm is something of divine and great spiritual importance. The energy generated should be treated with respect and used for some higher motive. How many people have sex in the West only to help them sleep?

Once we have established the importance of the orgasm we can concentrate on improving and sustaining it and, for men, increasing its frequency (not the ejaculatory type, of course). Someone once said that the orgasm is like lightning, lighting up the face of God for a split second. It makes sense then if we are practising tantric sex to learn how to turn that brief flash into a searchlight.

The physiological effects of orgasm

Before we go on to Chapter 6 let's spend some time thinking about what an orgasm is – what do you experience? How does your heartbeat change? What does your breathing do? Perhaps you could be slightly clinical about observing your own orgasm and seeing just exactly what physiological changes take place. And you could keep observing afterwards – what feelings do you have? How long does it take for everything to return to normal? How soon after orgasm do you want sex again? Does an orgasm, which is according to Western principles the peak of the sex act, make you want more or less of it?

EXERCISE 1

Bring each other to orgasm and stare into each other's eyes as you do so. If either tries to look away or shut the eyes the other should give a gentle reminder to 'stay here' or 'stay present'. This keeps you in touch with your body and allows you to experience the orgasm as a purely physical activity.

Later, when you have both recovered, you should bring each other to orgasm again. This time you are both allowed to shut your eyes if you want. You may find that you 'wander off alone' during your orgasm. Afterwards you can discuss how the orgasms varied each time.

Again later when you have recovered (this exercise can be done over three days if you want) you should bring each other to

orgasm. This time as you orgasm put the tip of your tongue on the roof of your mouth and close your eyes. Focus your eyes on the space behind and slightly above your eyebrows – the third eye – and watch what happens there. You could even try stopping your ears up – *listen* to what happens when you orgasm – and that doesn't mean the sound of your own voice.

Again you and your partner might like to compare notes about the different types of orgasm. The third type is more likely to bring you into contact with some form of spiritual experience. You may be able to think of ways to improve it for yourself.

EXERCISE 2

If you've worked your way through the exercises in Chapter 4, you should by now have a pretty good idea of each other's bodies and how to massage, stroke, soothe and caress each other. You should also be pretty efficient in knowing what turns your lover on. You can use all those skills in this exercise. You can caress each other up to but not beyond the point of orgasm. As you reach each peak just stop and let it subside. Treat this one as a game, a sort of competition – who can nearly reach orgasm the most times before actually having one? Who can bring the other nearest to the point without actually going over?

You can also do this one with yourself as the competitor. How close can you bring yourself? We often don't know the point of no return until we have practised it a few times. We often don't even know there is a cut-off point. And we rarely, if ever, deliberately try not to have an orgasm when we are having sex. Try these techniques and see what happens. If you and your partner practise on each other you may find that your bouts of sex increase in duration – you both last longer than before. You may find that without orgasm you enjoy the caresses more – or less. Tantric sex is an art form, a skill, an exact science. You are the experiment, the tapestry, the orchard to be planted – and no that's not me waxing lyrical but the words of an old Chinese Taoist.

Getting the hand brake off

When you know yourself well and your orgasm levels and requirements, you can handle your sexual experiences much better. It's a bit like learning to drive a car – you're having lessons. Yes, you could probably get the thing to go if no one showed you how it worked but you'd have to fumble around a bit, and you'd never really get out of first gear or even manage to get the hand brake off.

The equality of tantric sex

One of the really nice things about tantric sex is the equality it pays to each sex – men and women are both important to each other. Another good thing is the way it treats sex with respect; there are no crude words for parts of the body or encouragement to treat each other in a bad way, only respect and trust.

Chinese erotic manuals

The Taoist teachers were very aware that lovers have different moods and appetites for sex. They recommended that partners keep copies of some traditional Chinese erotic books by the bed and, if either lover seemed unresponsive or needed encouragement, then the lover who wanted to indulge in sex could bring out the book and lay it on the bed. Together they could then look through it and find the parts that were stimulating. The teachers were also aware that young brides often found it difficult to talk about sex or express what they wanted to do in an open and liberated way. This was often the case for shy young husbands as well.

The Chinese erotic books were heavily illustrated with explicit pictures and the lovers, sitting side by side, could get aroused just looking at the drawings. They could also tell what excited or interested their partners by how long they lingered on a particular

page, or they could even nudge each other and then both try what the other wanted. This could all be done without words and was a good way for young lovers both to express their desires without the embarrassment of speaking, to experiment together.

Realising how valuable these pictures were to inexperienced lovers the Taoist teachers didn't think of them as rude or pornographic as we might. The Chinese honeymooners would have looked through their erotic Taoist manuals together and learnt much about the techniques of lovemaking from them. And it would have been a very equal, shared experience since the artwork depicts scenes of love as much as sex.

The Taoist teachers were very aware of the importance of arousal. They suggested, and it can be seen in most aspects of Chinese erotic art, that partially clothed lovers are more arousing that completely nude ones, and that the removal or disarray of just one item of clothing is far more erotic and suggestive than entire nakedness.

The equal union of lovers

The teachers were also keen to point out that sex when one of the lovers wasn't ready or in the mood was pointless. Sex, to the Taoists, had to be a completely equal union of two lovers both entering into a relation together with the same degree of willingness. The thought of one partner having to be coerced or bullied into sex would have been abhorrent to them. Their idea of energy exchange was so intrinsic that they would have preferred not to have had sex at all rather than share energy with someone who resented it or who had been pressurised into it.

The energy of the Tao

The idea of energy exchange is not just a theory, it is a practical demonstrable part of sex. If you build up resentment and inhibition it will show in your lovemaking. A sensitive partner will quickly be

able to feel that something is wrong. That's why an integral part of Taoist foreplay was concerned with massage. By spending time intimately and gently caressing your partner's entire body before sex takes place you can build up a pretty good mental picture of the stresses, desires and tensions. If you feel you don't want to spend the time doing this, or would rather just 'get on with it' then the Taoists would have questioned your attitude to sex. They believed that satisfying your partner was more important than self-satisfaction. They believed this because, as your partner gains satisfaction and is comfortable and happy in life, the benefits spill over into everyday activities and those benefits also affect you. If your partner is unsatisfied or resentful sexually then that attitude will affect you.

The art of arousal

The massage before sex was an essential ingredient in pleasing lovers. By caressing away their cares and tensions they would relax and be more responsive. And likewise you, too, will be more aroused and ready for sex if you have a partner who spends some time beforehand soothing and caring for your body. Sex, to the Taoist, was a time spent together not just having intercourse but really together – loving, caressing, massaging, talking, caring and kissing. The actual sex part, as seen by the West, probably took up very little time, but the rest was to be enjoyed for quite a long session. Nothing was to be rushed or hurried. To the Taoists the Western notion of casual sex would be viewed as positively harmful because the energy wouldn't have had time to be fully generated.

The Taoists believed that the art of arousal was all important. To make love to someone who is not aroused is disrespectful and selfish. The erotic arts of arousal can be almost instinctively learnt if we remember the fundamental principles of yin and yang. The man, being yang and with all that implies (see page 43) needs a more visual system of arousal – the merest sight of an unclothed thigh can be erotic to a man, whereas a woman, being yin, needs a subtler form of arousal – intimate touching, emotional stroking and loving

suggestions will be more effective. Obviously there are lovers who will respond differently but the basic idea of yin and yang can be explored. The yang energy is faster to rise and cools quicker; the yin is slower but longer lasting, it is also deeper and more sustained, whereas the yang is quickly dispelled but faster to recharge.

6 THE MALE ORGASM

Man is Yang and quick as fire and dies down soon; woman is Yin and slow as water but, once roused, becomes the torrent.

Wang T'sieu

The yin cauldron and the yang furnace

We have already looked at the way the Taoists regard yin and yang energy, the male and female principles. Yang, the male principle, is the fire; while yin, the female principle, is water. Fire is quick and spontaneous and can be easily extinguished by water. The water is much slower to heat up but, once hot, takes much longer to cool down. Together they can be a powerful force. If you poured water over a fire it would just go out, but if you were to use the fire to heat the water in a pot then it would boil and could be used for cooking or washing or whatever other purpose you desired. This analogy of the cooking pot is Taoist. The woman is often described as the 'yin cauldron' and the man as the 'yang furnace'.

The peak of ching

The yin energy is said to reside in a woman's belly – the cauldron – while a man's fire resides in his testicles – the furnace. Once that fire

has briefly flared up in ejaculation he is extinguished until he has had time to recover. The Taoists believed that the male orgasm, known as the 'peak of ching' – ching being translated as 'spirit' – could be separate from his ejaculation. The yang spirit, ching, is said by Chinese medical practitioners to be stored in the kidneys. This spirit can be both physical – sperm – and ethereal – ch'i energy. Men who ejaculate at orgasm are losing both the physical and the spiritual type of ching. The Taoists recommended that the man tries to hold on to the physical part of ching as much as possible. Losing ching causes ill health, retaining ching promotes longevity and good health.

Retaining the seed

This orgasm without ejaculation is known as retaining the seed. It doesn't mean you can't orgasm. It only means that there is a distinct difference between orgasm and ejaculation. Once that concept is accepted the following exercises may become easier. Even if you don't manage the retaining of seed your efforts will not have been wasted – all the following exercises will enable you to have sex for much longer without orgasm, learn more about being a better and more considerate lover, and help you get and keep an erection more easily. None of these things will go unappreciated by your partner.

Controlling ejaculation

Whereas some of these exercises can be done by the man alone it will be assumed that he and his partner are practising tantric sex together and that neither one of you is more or less experienced than the other. If the true delights of tantric sex are to be learnt and enjoyed and used then all it takes is practice. In the West we tend to have sex when our passions are aroused or the opportunity presents itself or even out of habit. However, we are now studying Eastern practices and that means sex is a learning experience. A time and place has to be set aside when you and your partner can practise.

Booking sex

Mood and passion don't really play a part in this learning process. It may sound a little cold and clinical to 'book' a time for sex and to discuss beforehand which exercises you are going to do or which parts you are going to practise – but this is only for a while. Once you have learnt each other's rhythms, methods and means you can return to mood and passion with a new-found experience and wisdom that will more than compensate for the time spent 'in the classroom'. These 'training sessions' should also be fun. Make sure you are warm enough and that your surroundings are harmonious and conducive to good lovemaking.

EXERCISE 1

The Locking Position

The couple should have sex with passion and vigour and the man should ejaculate – then they are ready to begin. They should have sex again. This time the man, especially if he is young and sexually inexperienced, will be much less likely to orgasm quite so quickly the second time – or even third or fourth if he is full of ching. The man should be 'on top'. He should practise the 'thrusts of the heron'. This is where he pushes his 'jade hammer', penis, into the woman's 'jade gate', vulva, three times deeply and then once quite shallow. This will enable him to almost withdraw his jade hammer on the fourth or shallow stroke if he feels himself about to orgasm. As he almost withdraws he should arch his back and 'suck' in his lower abdomen. This is known as the 'locking' position and it should help him avoid orgasm. Obviously he must be aware of how close he is and not leave it too late. The thrusts of the heron can go on for as long as he likes unless he feels the imminence of orgasm, when he should carry out the locking position. When the feeling of near orgasm has subsided he can continue with the heron thrusts.

ThRUSTS OF ThE ÒRAGON

Once you are experienced with the heron thrusts you might like to move on to the 'thrusts of a dragon'. This is where the man thrusts deeply nine times and then once quite shallow. Again he should carry out the locking position if he feels an orgasm coming on.

Once mastered, the thrusts of a dragon can be reversed for the 'thrusts of the phoenix'. This is where the man thrusts very shallow for nine strokes and then once very deeply. Women who have never been able to have a vaginal orgasm report that the phoenix thrusts are often the very movements that enable them to have one for the first time.

Modern sexologists often suggest that the man should not think about sex if he wants to retain ejaculation control but should instead count or recite something or even, believe it or not, work out his monthly bills. However we are learning tantric sex techniques and no such advice would ever be given here. The man, if he suffers from premature ejaculation, would be much better off learning the locking method which would both help him and certainly go a long way towards giving his partner pleasure and satisfaction. You could always concentrate on the texture of your partner's hair or the quality of her skin, but be present, be there in the act as much as possible. Counting and bill paying are nothing to do with sex.

EXERCISE 2

ThE SQUEEZE TEChNIQUE

The couple should have sex in the same way as described for Exercise 1. The same techniques of the heron, dragon and phoenix thrusts can be used. When the man feels he is reaching orgasm, instead of withdrawing his jade hammer he should use his index and forefinger to press quite hard on his perineum – the small area situated between the scrotum and the anus – the

site of his base chakra. Obviously different men will need different pressure, and only *you* can find out how much you need. But sufficient pressure should be used so that the orgasm subsides. The first few times you try this you may even lose your erection but this is only because the technique is new. Once you've done it a few times you will be able to maintain your erection quite easily.

The main difference between the locking method and the 'squeeze' method as it is known is that the man can quite easily do it himself without disturbing his partner's rhythm. His partner can obviously do the squeezing for him if the couple prefer.

Once the methods in these two exercises are learnt, ejaculation control can become an easier concept to deal with. It also makes it much more satisfying for the woman as her partner will be able to keep his thrusting up indefinitely.

The art of a thousand thrusts

The ancient Taoist love texts suggested that a man was quite capable of a thousand thrusts without once feeling the need to orgasm. However, this may be a bit of Taoist bravado. But any increase must be beneficial – especially for his partner.

Cautions

The tantric texts also suggest that none of these things should be done too quickly. If you have been used to making love every night and always ejaculating, your body is obviously going to be used to making lots of sperm. If you suddenly stop you may experience some tightness or discomfort in the scrotum so phase it in slowly. Some men also experience a feeling of exhaustion if they don't ejaculate as frequently as normal when they initially start this technique. Try having sex and not ejaculating only every other time to begin with.

The plateau of delight

Once the lock and squeeze is mastered the man may start to experience the 'plateau of delight'. This wonderful expression is a Taoist way of describing the ejaculate-less orgasm. This is where the man has all the sensations of the orgasm without the emission. And the plateau of delight can be experienced as many times as he likes because there is no loss of energy accompanying it. The plateau of delight is also just that – a plateau – which implies, quite correctly, that you can continue to go higher and experience still more pleasure, without reaching a peak.

More thrusts

Once all this is mastered the man might like to incorporate some other thrusts into his love play.

- **Wild horse thrusts** – the man bucks and thrusts wildly, always going in deeply like a wild horse fording a river.

- **Snake thrusts** – the man pushes in quite deeply but very slowly.

- **Mouse thrusts** – very quick and very shallow.

- **Eagle thrusts** – the man holds his jade hammer for a while, motionless, at the entrance to the jade gate then, like an eagle swooping after its prey, he thrusts very quickly.

- **Sparrow thrusts** – very shallow, teasing around the entrance to the jade gate.

- **Ox thrusts** – alternate deep and shallow but very slow and ponderous, like an ox.

- **Bear thrusts** – the man makes very deep thrusts but holds his jade hammer in as far as it will go and for as long as possible.

You might like to experiment with your own variations on these.

PC muscle

The pubococcygeus muscle is known as the PC muscle. So where is it and what's it for? When you are urinating try to stop halfway through. You use the PC muscle to stop the flow. In Taoist tantra they recommend that the man should clench and unclench his PC muscle every day at least seventy-five times. It's located just above the perineum and if you exercise it, it helps ejaculation control as well as improving blood supply and general muscle tone.

The Testicle Dance

If you stand nude in front of a mirror you should be able to see your penis twitch slightly upright when you exercise the PC muscle. If you want to undergo the rather vigorous training required you could, just by clenching the PC muscle have an erection to order whenever you wanted. You could, and this is really extreme tantric stuff, do the testicle dance. If you clench the PC you'll notice that one testicle will rise very slightly. With constant practice you'll be able to get it to rise considerably. Some of the more extreme tantric cults would tie weights on to the testicles and then lift them off the ground just by clenching the PC muscle. Apparently the maximum weight possible is about 1 kilogram (2 lbs) but I don't think you'll find it in the *Guinness Book of Records*.

Make 'em laugh

When you are making love with your partner you can try clenching the PC muscle and see what effect it has. You can also use it to prevent ejaculation – it's a bit like the squeeze technique but done internally. And if you want a bit of fun and to entertain your partner you can put a towel or similar cloth on your erect penis and get it to jump by clenching the PC muscle. It doesn't do anything sexy but it will probably make her laugh.

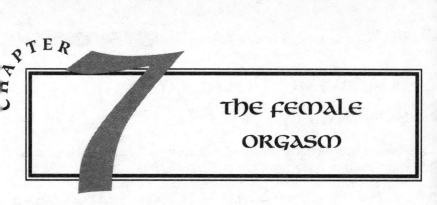

THE FEMALE ORGASM

So let us praise and exalt Him who has created woman and her beauties, with her appetising flesh; who has given her hair, a beautiful figure, a bosom with breasts which are swelling, and amorous ways, which awaken desires.

The Perfumed Garden

FEEDING MALE ENERGY

We looked at the male orgasm from the Taoist point of view in Chapter 6. In this chapter we will do the same for the female orgasm. There are some important fundamental differences which tie in with the way the Taoists look at the energy of the different sexes. According to Taoist theory, women's yin energy is darker, cooler and deeper. It is capable of 'feeding' male energy without being depleted because there is simply so much of it. But a woman's yin energy does need the spark of fire of the male yang energy sometimes to 'kick start' it into life. That's the wonderful thing about tantric sex: both sides of the couple are needed – the male and the female – the yin and the yang. Without the other both are less, but together, (and it is more than just the combined power of two energy systems) they combine into the power of the universe – the Tao itself – the Supreme Ultimate.

In the tantric texts there is no restriction put on the number, frequency or intensity of female orgasms, unlike the male. There is no 'seed' for women to retain, therefore they can feel free to enjoy, explore and experiment with their sexuality as much as possible.

Knowing your own sexuality

Firstly a woman has to know what that sexuality means. She should know her own body, how it responds, what it is capable of, how to train it, what that training consists of, what to expect for her sexuality and, most importantly, how she can channel that sexuality towards a higher purpose – that of spirituality, which is what tantric sex is all about.

Liberated Lovers

Because of the way most Western women are brought up, their sexual nurturing has been less than that of the East where women are taught from an early age how to improve and enjoy their lovemaking. In the West there can often be a barrier, either mental or moral, that women experience when it comes to *enjoying* their sexuality. This barrier has to be removed before women can take their true and rightful place as liberated, fully sexual, empowered and satisfied lovers. The practice of tantric sex is a great help in removing that barrier. If enjoying sex was only about enjoying sex then it would not be so helpful; but when you give it a spiritual purpose then it somehow becomes acceptable – you are not just a lover but also a lover of God, a *Shakti*, a living representation of the female deity on Earth, and that's a powerful responsibility – don't let Her down.

The different types of orgasm

The tantric texts have always recognised that women play an important part in sex and that they are 'special' by nature of the fact that they can have several different types of orgasm. In the next exercise we will explore those different types and how to achieve them.

EXERCISE 1

SELF-EXPLORATION

For a lot of women in the West an intimate knowledge of their own bodies is something frowned on – it's just not nice. But how can you be the consort of Shiva if you are shy or coy? By exploring our own bodies we learn how they work, when we know how they work we can use that information to help our lover please us and to please him as well.

Whereas the tantric texts frown on male masturbation, they regard female masturbation as worthwhile, even to be recommended. The yin energy has to be dissipated at times when your lover is not there. And by knowing your orgasm well you can relax and enjoy the spiritual aspect without having to worry about technique or false expectations. Begin by knowing the different types of orgasm and how you respond to them.

THE CLITORAL ORGASM

The clitoris is located just in front of and above the vaginal opening. The tantras call it by various names including the 'lotus bud' and the 'jade pearl'. When stroked and caressed by you or your lover it will bring you to orgasm. Feel that orgasm – how does it manifest throughout your body? Just as you orgasm try panting vigorously, does it delay or enhance your orgasm? Can you always achieve a clitoral orgasm? Do you need a special time of day? Is your libido lower in the mornings? Where do you go in your mind when you are masturbating? Can you masturbate freely in front of your lover? There are no right or wrong answers.

THE VAGINAL ORGASM

As its name implies it is brought about by internal stimulation but how does it feel to you? Is it different from your clitoral orgasm? Can you achieve the vaginal orgasm? Most research suggests that a lot of women need a much longer period of

internal stimulation than their male lovers are capable of for them to experience the vaginal orgasm. This is why it's important for men to learn the techniques in Chapter 6, and to be more considerate of their partner's cooler, slower-to-rouse energy.

The G-SPOT ORGASM

Most people think the G-spot is a recent invention or discovery – but it's not. The tantric texts talk about the 'hidden jade moon' or the 'heart of the lotus bud'. The G-spot is to be found about an inch or two inside the vulva on the top wall; it's a small area with a slightly rougher feel to it. Perhaps a good way to find it is to think of it as the underside of the clitoris – the yin or hidden side of the yang or external clitoris. Some women report no extra sensation here while others recommend it as an area to be stimulated for orgasm. And the orgasm induced by G-spot stimulation is different from the other two types. If a woman's lover is considerate and skilful he may be able to stimulate the G-spot with the head of his penis. This is why a lot of the techniques you will find in Chapter 8 involve the man making turning or twisting movements with his penis; it affords extra stimulation above and beyond the normal thrusting that most men seem to think is their only option.

ALL THREE

Some women, and again it may depend on the patience and skill of their lovers, claim that it is possible to have three orgasms simultaneously: one in each of the three areas. You may like to try this, although it's best not to be 'goal oriented' or you may miss the journey. Once we start setting 'targets' we open ourselves up to disappointment and false expectations. However, as an exercise it's useful to know what sort of ultimate is possible; this lets us know what we are capable of. If the male lover is skilful he may be able to use his penis to stimulate the vaginal orgasm and, at the same time, using his thumb and index finger stimulate both the clitoris and G-spot. Some women also report an anal orgasm if their sphincter muscles are stimulated gently.

Nectar of the moon

The Taoist texts also suggest that a woman is capable of a sort of internal ejaculation. This seems to be a very moist flow from the vulva at the point of orgasm. Some women produce copious fluid at that moment while others don't. The Taoists called this the 'nectar of the moon' and regarded it as most beneficial for men to taste as it was the most highly charged yin essence that they could absorb. The Taoists called saliva the 'jade spring' and also recommended that men could taste that and absorb the yin essence from it.

The PC muscle

For the woman, development of the PC muscle (pubococcygeus muscle) will be most useful. To first find it and experience it the woman should insert one finger into the vagina and grip that finger with her vaginal muscles. That muscle action is the PC muscle being used. Once you have felt it, it should be easy to tighten and relax it with practice. The tantric texts recommend flexing it at least seventy-five times a day both to strengthen it and to learn to control it. Once it has developed it should be capable of gripping quite strongly. Your lover will benefit from the stimulating effect it can have; by tightening it and relaxing it you should be able to squeeze him to orgasm without moving any other parts of you. Strengthening the PC muscle is especially beneficial to women after childbirth. Some women who have practised tantric sex for a long time claim to be able to set up a series of 'ripple' actions in their vaginas that can be most stimulating for their partner; the same ripple action that a woman can perform with her mouth and throat when she is stimulating her partner orally.

Communication

Some women find it quite hard to orgasm during intercourse and need stimulating by hand or orally. This should be incorporated into

your lovemaking so that your lover doesn't feel he's 'letting you down' or not 'good enough'. In early chapters we talked about tantric sex being about communication. If you don't tell your partner what you want and need he will not be able to read your mind. There are some tantric lovers who seem to know instinctively what a woman requires but they are usually very experienced in Eastern love techniques and have worked with the energy of sex for years. You and your partner may well be just starting out. If you are new to this form of sex then it's only fair to give him some encouragement and help. You will have to go slowly and explain clearly what you need and want, and then he will get more skilled and that will benefit both of you. You have to remember that Western sexual technique education for both men and women is usually non-existent. Most men are hot impulsive lovers who have to work hard to become considerate patient partners; that's not because they are ill-mannered or rude or selfish – it's merely that they don't know any different; they've never been shown or taught that there is an alternative. Once shown they will never go back to their old way of loving. But you have to tell them what is needed.

Oral Loving

When a man loves your vulva with his lips, mouth and tongue he is worshipping the female deity – you are the Shakti and you are feeding his energy. Good oral sex takes time and patience – you will have to communicate again: tell him what pressure you like, where and how to move his tongue, which bits to suck on, where to blow softly. Teach him how to use his fingers inside you at the same time as licking your clitoris. And if you want really long sessions of oral sex then just hold his penis while he loves you; most men get to feel remote and cut off if there is no penile stimulation while they are loving you. If you hold them the energy is completing a circuit.

Bear in mind that during sex you have a role to play – as does your partner. Your role is to feed his energy so he can go on loving you for as long as you need. If he has an orgasm he may find that the

energy dissipates completely for a while and he will need to rest, perhaps even to sleep, to recover that energy. His role is to orchestrate and be active; your role is to participate and be creative. He worships your Shakti; you feed his Shiva. Without one the other is lessened; together you are a powerful force. You will be able to maintain your levels of energy better if you are aware of your partner's need to orgasm and you should delay this as long as possible. If he is learning the lock method or the squeeze technique outlined in Chapter 6 then it's in your own best interests to help him as much as possible. Women often, quite rightly, complain that their lover is too quick, or doesn't spend enough time on foreplay, then they do everything in their power to make their lover orgasm quickly. It makes sense to help them delay the male orgasm. You will be able to have as many orgasms as you like and, each time you do, you are feeding your lover's energy. Once he has ejaculated, his energy level plummets. If he is learning and practising the ejaculate-less orgasm you will together be able to reach new heights of pleasure.

In the next chapter we will learn how to put everything we have learnt so far together and have really great tantric sex.

8

THE POSITIONS OF GOOD SEX

The languishing eye
Connects soul with soul
And the tender kiss
Takes the message from member to vulva

The Perfumed Garden

THE TANTRIC TRADITIONS

In this chapter we will look at how the three great tantric traditions – the Hindu, the Arabic and the Taoist – looked at the positions for good sex. These positions weren't described and recommended for titillation or to teach lovers how to be contortionists: they were there for lovers to experiment and to find positions that were comfortable so they could enjoy each other's energy for a long time. They were also described so that lovers could find positions where they could embrace and caress each other better or more intimately. These positions may seem to be about sex but they are actually more about love; you have to have a loving and trusting partner with whom to work through them.

Let's begin by looking at the *Kama Sutra*. This ancient Hindu text suggests that there are sixty-four different lovemaking positions, but on close inspection it turns out that there are only twenty-three with each having many variations depending on how deep the *lingam* (penis) is thrust into the *yoni* (vulva) or the manner in which it is moved. The *Kama Sutra* also deals in some depth with oral sex which we will look at later.

The twenty-three basic positions of the Kama Sutra

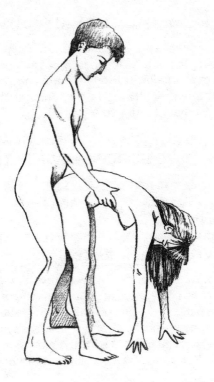

The Congress of the Cow

POSITIONS WITH THE MAN BEHIND

The Congress of the Cow

The word congress is used in the *Kama Sutra* for 'intercourse' or, more properly 'meeting'. In the Congress of the Cow the couple should have sex in the manner brought to mind by the title of this position. The woman stands upright and bends forward until her

hands touch the ground. The man then enters her from behind and clasps her around the waist much as a bull would mount a cow. In this position he can also stimulate her clitoris and his pelvic bone will be able to stimulate the area around her buttocks and perineum.

The Congress of the Elephant

This is not quite so obvious from its title, however the woman lies face down and the man enters her from behind with his legs outside hers. He should support his weight on his arms. The woman, by pressing her thighs tightly together, should be able to provide extra friction for the man if required.

POSITIONS WITH THE COUPLE STANDING UP

The Congress of the Vine (or The Supported Congress)

The couple have sex standing up with the man leaning back against a wall for support. The woman should entwine her legs around the back of the man's thighs. It's probably best if she tries this with only one leg at a time unless he is very strong or she is very athletic. If the couple are of very different heights the man should bend his knees and keep his legs apart so he can lower himself to the woman's level.

The Congress of the Monkey (or The Suspended Congress)

The man leans back against a wall for support and the woman clasps him around the neck. If he bends his knees she will be able to grip the back of his thighs with her heels and use her toes against the wall for extra thrust. The man should grip the woman around her upper thighs to support her. Both this position and the preceding one need some strength and practise but are good for spontaneous sex and indulging in erotic kissing.

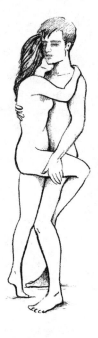

Congress of the Vine

POSITIONS WITH THE WOMAN ON TOP

The Pair of Tongs

The man lies down and the woman sits astride him, facing him, with her knees bent back. There need be no thrusting if the woman has practised her PC muscle exercises; she can just gently squeeze his lingam. The man, in this position, can caress the woman's breasts and she can stimulate her own clitoris – or the man can.

The Spinning Top

Here the couple begin as the Pair of Tongs but the woman slowly, and carefully, swivels around until she is facing away from the man. This one is both difficult, and potentially painful for the man. Take great care. The woman can swivel back again into the Pair of Tongs.

The Swing

The man sits half upright and the woman sits in his lap facing away from him. She should support her weight by gripping his ankles and the man should support his own weight by propping himself up on his arms. In this position the woman can, as the name suggests, swing herself backwards and forwards, or even from side to side.

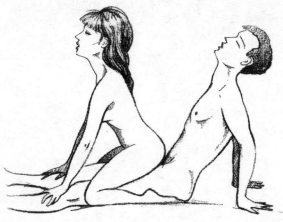

The Swing

The Congress of The Mare

The woman sits as in The Swing, in the man's lap while he is sitting half upright. Instead of leaning forwards she leans back. The man should take his weight on his arms. This should leave the woman free to stimulate her clitoris and the man can kiss her neck and shoulders.

The Woman Sitting Astride the Man

Maybe a better suggestion than the Spinning Top is to get into a position where the woman sits astride the man, facing away, and inserts his lingam into her yoni.

If the woman grips her partner's ankles she can then exert considerable pressure and friction on his lingam while still maintaining control. Some women find the Spinning Top quite tiring and some men find it painful because the woman's weight on his upper thighs can be restrictive. However, it is a fun position to try and can be very stimulating. The *Kama Sutra* recommends it for couples who have been together for a long time as each, being unable to see the face of their partner, can fantasise that they are making love to a stranger – or someone else they desire.

The *Kama Sutra* says:

> *Though a woman is reserved, and keeps her feelings hidden, when she mounts her man from above she can show all her love and desire, and from her actions a man should be able to tell what disposition she is in and in what way she likes to be enjoyed.*

POSITIONS WITH THE MAN ON TOP

The Widely Opened Congress

The couple start in the classic 'man on top' position with the woman's knees outside his thighs. She should then arch her back and he should support his weight on his knees and arms. The woman's buttocks should not be in contact with whatever is underneath her. The woman, by opening her legs as wide as possible, should be able to enjoy very deep penetration and good stimulation of her clitoris by the man's pelvic region.

The Yawning Congress

The woman lies down and raises and opens her legs as wide as possible. The man kneels between her legs and enters her. The couple should clasp hands to support each other's weight. The woman's inner thighs should grip around the man's waist.

The Highest Yawning Congress

The couple should take up the Yawning Congress and then the woman should bring her knees forwards to rest on her breasts. The man can then straighten out his legs and take his weight on his arms. The woman can rest her feet on his shoulders. This position provides the deepest penetration.

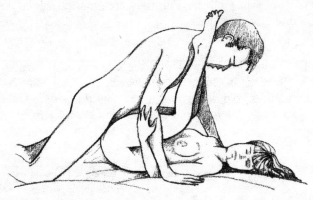

The Highest Yawning Congress

The Congress of the Consort of Indra

Indra was the Hindu god of Thunder and this may have been his favourite position – or that of his consort or wife. The woman lies down on her back and brings her knees together tightly on her breasts. The man kneels and enters her. She can then rest her feet on his stomach while he grips the back of her thighs or, in this position, he can stimulate her clitoris extremely well. For added tension she can grip her shins and pull her knees even more tightly against her breasts.

The Clasping Position

The woman lies down and the man enters her by lying on top of her. She entwines her legs with his and their arms also entwine. This position doesn't allow for much movement but it is a very intimate warm embrace.

The Side Clasping Position

The couple lie on their sides facing each other. The woman lifts one leg to allow the man to enter her. They can entwine legs and arms or use their hands to caress each other.

The Twining Congress

The couple adopt the classic 'man on top' position. The woman should bring one leg around the back of her partner's thighs and draw him closer to her. At the same time she should clasp him around the neck and draw his head down to hers.

The Pressing Congress

The same as the Twining Congress but the woman uses both her legs to press even harder against the man's thighs. Her feet should grip quite hard behind his knees.

The Rising Congress

The woman should lie down on her back and draw her knees up to her breasts. The man kneels and enters her. He should then grip her legs and bring them up so that her feet are on his shoulders. He will need to open his thighs quite wide to enable him to penetrate her deeply. This position is quite tiring for the man although it does afford the woman considerable pleasure due to its deep penetration.

The Pressed Congress

This position is very similar to the Congress of the Consort of Indra, but instead of the woman gripping her legs tightly to her she can relax her knees. The man can caress her feet and she can stroke his thighs.

The Half Pressed Congress

The woman can relax one leg completely by stretching it out behind her partner. This lets him have access to her clitoris which he can then stimulate with his fingers.

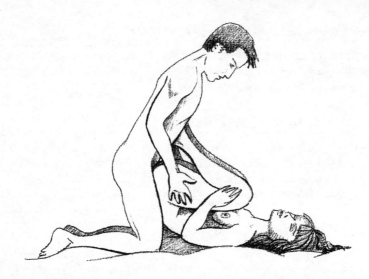

The Pressed Congress

The Nailed Half Press Congress

From the previous position the woman can take the foot that is on the man's chest and lift her leg completely into the air. At the same time the man should extend one leg behind him.

The Congress of the Crab

The woman lies on her back with her legs widely apart and her knees drawn up. The man kneels and enters her. He clasps her knees to his chest. She can then let her legs down and draw them up again. If she does this quickly and smoothly he will gain a lot of pleasure from the tightening and relaxing of her yoni.

The Lotus Congress

Not even to be attempted unless you are both very supple and energetic.

The woman lies on her back with her knees drawn up so that she is in the full lotus position but lying down. The man enters her by crouching over her on all fours.

You were warned you had to be supple and energetic!

The Bamboo Congress

The man enters the woman who is lying on her back. He extends one leg behind him and she brings one leg up so that her foot is resting on his shoulder – this should be the opposite leg to the one he has extended. By alternately raising and lowering a leg in the woman's case, or bringing one back and forth in the man's case, they can bring themselves to orgasm.

This position is supposed to resemble bamboo being split. It's not easy and only really included so you can try it for fun.

Movements of the Lingam

Once the twenty-three positions are learnt, or even during the learning process, the man can also learn how to move his penis to afford the woman maximum satisfaction. The *Kama Sutra* is very clear in its advice to men – your role is to satisfy the woman; unless you learn to be a patient, sympathetic and considerate lover you cannot attain the true tantra.

Movements of the Lingam during Lovemaking

- **The Moving Forward** The lingam is inserted into the yoni in a straightforward manner and pushed fully home.
- **The Sporting of the Sparrow** The lingam is moved in and out rapidly in tiny movements like a sparrow.
- **The Blows of the Bull and Bear** The lingam is rubbed against the side of the vaginal walls.
- **The Giving of a Blow** The lingam is used to strike the outside of the yoni – especially effective if struck against the clitoris.

- **The Pressing**   The lingam is used to rub hard against the outside of the yoni – again it works well if the clitoris is stimulated by the lingam.

- **The Rubbing**   The lingam is inserted and pushed hard against the 'bottom' of the yoni – the vaginal wall on the opposite side to the clitoris.

- **The Piercing**   This is the same as the Rubbing except the lingam is rubbed hard against the 'top' of the yoni – the vaginal wall where the G-spot is situated.

- **The Churning**   The lingam is used inside the yoni and is 'churned' about, rubbing against the vaginal walls.

You might like to experiment with your own variations of these – and invent names for them.

ORAL SEX

The *Kama Sutra* gives advice to a man on how to give oral sex to a woman – it says the man should follow the same advice as for kissing. Perhaps you'd better refer to Chapter 3 if you've not been practising erotic kissing.

For the woman there is also helpful advice about oral sex. The *Kama Sutra* suggests that there is an eight-fold path to *Auparishtaka* or mouth-congress:

- **Nominal Congress**   The lingam is caressed by the woman's mouth.

- **Biting the Sides**   The lingam is held by the woman and her teeth can gently nibble along the sides.

- **Outside Pressing**   The head of the lingam is sucked gently by the woman's lips.

- **Inside Pressing**   The whole of the lingam is inserted into the woman's mouth and she gives long deep sucks with her whole mouth.

- **Kissing**   The lingam is kissed all over by the woman.

- **Tongueing**   The lingam is fiercely licked all over by the woman's tongue.
- **Sucking the Mango Fruit**   About half of the lingam is inserted into the woman's mouth and she should suck hard in the same manner as the Inside Pressing.
- **Swallowing Up**   The whole of the lingam is taken into the mouth and sucked hard with a deep swallow motion.

The Congress of the Crow

If the couple want to engage in mutual oral sex they should adopt **The Congress of the Crow**. This equates with the classic '69' position of Western sex practices. Here the couple can engage in mutual caressing of the genitals in comfort.

The Congress of the Crow

The Ananga Ranga

The *Ananga Ranga* offers only a few variations on the positions given in the *Kama Sutra* but it does offer one excellent variation of the 'woman on top' position.

The Large Bee Position

The woman sits astride the man, with his lingam entered into her yoni. She closes her legs in front of her and grasps his lingam tightly.

She can then lean back and take her own weight on her arms – even gripping his ankles with her hands if she wants to and it feels comfortable. She can then begin a series of twisting movements from the waist down – this is the large bee. The advice given in the tantric text is that she shouldn't be too aggressive or masculine in her movements as it will upset her partner's ego. However, modern lovers shouldn't have to worry too much about that and the woman can let go to all her desires at this stage. Most women find this position extremely comfortable and they can maintain it for quite a long time.

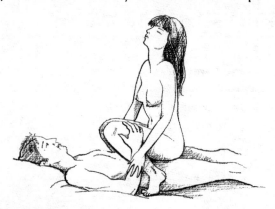

The Large Bee Position

The woman's orgasm

The woman may like to experiment by moving her legs forwards or backwards until the optimum position for comfort and friction is found. Basically the man has to lie back and enjoy his partner doing all the work. As a man you might like to thrust your hips upwards at the same time as your partner moves her waist from side to side. The man can caress his partner's breasts and she can stimulate her clitoris at the same time. If the simultaneous orgasm is important to you both then this is probably the best position to achieve it. The woman can bring herself to clitoral orgasm at the same time as the man ejaculates and she should be able to control the speed and pace much more sensitively in this position.

If the woman has mastered the yonic squeeze technique (PC muscle) then she may well be able to bring her partner to orgasm without moving any part of her body except the yoni.

The Perfumed Garden

There are eleven main lovemaking positions featured in *The Perfumed Garden*. Some of them are variations on positions we have already looked at. They are simply described as 'Manner the First', 'Manner the Second' and so forth. *The Perfumed Garden* does say that the positions that the Indian peoples use are more varied and better and goes on to describe them. We will look at these later.

Manner the First

The woman lies down on her back with her thighs raised. The man kneels between her legs and 'introduces his member into her'. He presses his toes into the ground and can then 'rummage her in a convenient, measured way'. This position is said to be gentle for the woman whose partner has a 'long measure'.

Manner the Second

The woman lies on her back and lifts her legs into the air and brings her legs as near her head as she can. The man then kneels and enters her. This position is said to be good if the man has a 'short measure' as it will afford the woman a degree of satisfaction.

Manner the Second

MANNER THE THIRD

The woman lies down and the man enters her from the kneeling position. She raises one leg only over his shoulder. This position will enable the couple to enjoy really deep penetration.

MANNER THE FOURTH

The woman lies down and the man enters her from the kneeling position. He then raises her legs up so that they are over his shoulders and he can grip her thighs as he thrusts deeply.

MANNER THE FIFTH

Both partners lie down on their sides, facing each other. This position is good for generating feelings of warmth and love; it is very intimate.

MANNER THE SIXTH

The woman kneels on all fours and then lowers her head to the ground. The man kneels behind her and enters her.

MANNER THE SEVENTH

The woman lies on her side and the man squats between her thighs with one of her legs on his shoulders and the other between his thighs. The man can then draw her to him by using his hands.

MANNER THE EIGHTH

The woman lies down on her back with her legs crossed at the knees. The man sits astride her like 'a cavalier on horseback' and, being on his knees, can 'put his member into her'.

MANNER THE NINTH

The woman kneels forward being propped up on a bed or raised couch. The man kneels behind her and enters her from behind. The man can keep his legs either side of hers.

MANNER THE TENTH

The woman half lies on a low couch so that the bottom half of her body is unsupported. The man kneels in front of her and enters her. She can then use her legs around his waist to support her and he can lean forwards and grip the low couch for support.

Manner the Tenth

MANNER THE ELEVENTH

The woman lies down on her back with a cushion under her buttocks. The man lies astride her and enters her. She should then cross her ankles over just behind and below his knees – or she can get her feet to meet together, sole to sole.

THE TWENTY-FIVE SUPERIOR INDIAN LOVEMAKING POSITIONS

The Perfumed Garden then goes on to describe the twenty-five positions of Indian lovemaking which it claims are superior to the Arabic tradition. It also warns that these shouldn't be tried by ill or unfit couples.

The Stopperage

The woman lies on her back with a cushion under her buttocks and the man enters her from the front. He should keep his legs outstretched and she should bend her legs up so that her knees are on his chest. *The Perfumed Garden* says this position can be uncomfortable for the woman and should only really be tried if the man's member is short or soft.

Frog Fashion

The woman lies on her back with her knees raised but her feet flat on the floor. The man sits with his legs around her sides. He enters her and holds on with his hands to her shoulders. Her knees should be under the man's armpits.

With The Toes Cramped

The woman lies on her back and the man kneels and enters her from the front. He should then grip with his toes and pull her up off the ground so that her buttocks can swing freely on to the front of his thighs. Her legs can then cross behind his back and he can grip her neck with his hands.

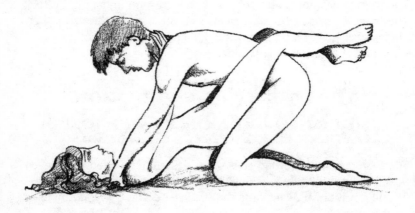

With The Toes Cramped

With Legs In The Air

The woman lies on her back and the man kneels and enters her from the front. Her legs should then be supported on his shoulders and he can lean forwards.

He-Goat Fashion

The woman crouches on her side and she stretches out the leg that is underneath. The man squats down between her thighs with his calves bent under him. He then lifts her uppermost leg so that it rests on his back and enters her. During this position he can take hold of the woman by her shoulders for extra leverage.

The Screw Of Archimedes

The man lies down on his back and the woman sits on him, facing him. She should then lean forwards and take her weight on her arms, positioned either side of his head. She can then slide up and down his member and, if he is agile, he can assist her by moving as well.

The Somersault

This position is really only for the very supple and very agile. The woman lies on her back with her legs up, one foot placed either side of her head and the man lies along her and enters her. It's called the somersault because it was originally recommended that to get into this position the woman should wear a pair of 'pantaloons' which she should drop so that they fit around her ankles. She should then bend forwards and put her head in them and the man should then seize her legs and somersault her into this position.

The Tail Of The Ostrich

The woman lies on her back and the man kneels in front of her and lifts up her legs until only her head and shoulders remain in contact with the ground. He then enters her, from behind, and straightens his back so that he is kneeling upright. She can then cross her ankles behind his head.

The Tail Of The Ostrich

FITTING ON OF THE SOCK

The man kneels down and the woman lies with her legs open and either side of his waist. He can lean back on his calves. He should then be able to use his member to stimulate the area around her vulva. In this position he can use his fingers to stimulate her clitoris as well. *The Perfumed Garden* says that:

when her vulva gets moistened with the liquid emitted from his verge she is thus amply prepared for enjoyment by the alternate coming and going of your weapon in her scabbard; put it into her in full length.

RECIPROCAL SIGHT OF THE POSTERIORS

The man lies stretched out on his back and the woman sits down on his member with her back to him. He can press the outside of her thighs between his thighs and legs while she places her hands on the ground as a support.

Reciprocal Sight Of The Posteriors

The Rainbow Arch

The woman lies on her side with one leg raised. The man lies also on his side with his face towards her back. He then enters her and keeps his hands on her back. She can then reach forwards and grip his feet and bring them forwards towards her front forming him into an arch.

The Alternate Movement Of Piercing

The man sits with his legs outstretched and the woman sits facing him in his lap. He then draws his legs up under her thighs and she grips his back with her legs. He should hold her round the waist and she can support herself by leaning back on her arms. All he has to do then is move his feet together to provide all the movement and friction they will require.

Pounding On The Spot

The same basic position as the Alternate Movement of Piercing except the man keeps his legs stretched out and the woman grips him tighter round the back.

Coitus From The Back

The woman lies face down and the man enters her from behind. He should keep his legs outstretched and inside hers. She should place a cushion or pillow under her so that her buttocks are raised.

Belly To Belly

The couple stand facing each other. He brings one leg forwards and she raises one leg. He should then be able to enter her quite easily. Both the partners should have their arms around each other's hips.

After The Fashion Of The Ram

The woman is on her knees with her forearms on the ground. The man kneels behind her and enters her and places his hands on her shoulders.

Driving The Peg Home

The woman leans back against a wall and the man enters her from the front. She takes her weight on her back and raises her legs, which she should lock around the back of his thighs. She can give herself additional support by holding on to his shoulders. He can then 'drive the peg home'.

Love's Fusion

While the woman is lying on her right side, the man should lie on his left with his left leg extended. The man's right leg should be raised until it is up to her flank when he then places her upper leg on his side. *The Perfumed Garden* then says 'after having introduced your member you move as you please, and she responds to your action as she pleases.'

Coitus Of The Sheep

The woman is on her hands and knees; the man, behind her, lifts her thighs until her vulva is on a level with his member, which he then inserts. In this position she ought to place her head between her arms.

Interchange In Coition

The man lies on his back. The woman, gliding in between his legs, places herself upon him with her toenails against the ground. She lifts up the man's thighs so he can enter her. She can then take her weight on her hands which she places either side of the man's body. *The Perfumed Garden* says this is an exact opposite of our traditional 'missionary position' and that a variation is for the woman to kneel with her legs under her but between his legs.

The Race Of The Member

The man, on his back, supports himself with a cushion under his shoulders but with his buttocks on whatever is underneath him. He then draws up his thighs until his knees are on a level with his face.

The woman then sits on him, 'impaling herself on his member; she must not lie down but keep seated as if on horseback, the saddle being represented by the knees and the stomach of the man'. All she has to do then is jog up and down by flexing her knees to bring them both to orgasm.

The Fitter In

The man sits with his legs apart and the woman sits between them. He enters her and they grip each other's elbows or forearms. Her legs should be around his waist and all four feet should be on the ground. They can then rock gently back and forth.

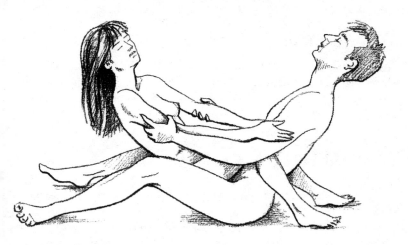

The Fitter In

The One Who Stops At Home

The woman lies down on her back with her shoulders and upper back supported by cushions. She arches her back and brings her feet back so that her knees are raised. She opens her legs and the man can half-kneel and enter her. She then raises and drops her buttocks to provide excitement and friction, but the man has to

follow her movements or his member will become dislodged – he has to 'stick like glue to her'.

The Coition Of The Blacksmith

The woman lies on her back with a cushion under her buttocks and her knees raised as far as possible towards her chest so that her vulva stands out as a target. She then guides her partner's member in. He then

executes for some time coition in the usual manner then draws his tool out of the vulva, and glides it for a moment between the thighs of the woman, as the smith withdraws the glowing iron from the furnace in order to plunge it into cold water.

The Seducer

The woman lies on her back, the man sits between her legs. She can then draw her legs up around his shoulders and guide his member in. She can clasp her legs around his waist if that is more comfortable.

Positions from the Tao

The Chinese tantric texts give all the positions that we have so far looked at but really only divide positions into four kinds; man on top, woman on top, couple side by side (and face to face), and man from behind. They called these 'Yang Superior', 'Yin Superior', 'Intimate Attachment' and 'Fish Sunning Itself'. They suggested that lovemaking should be fluid and versatile; there being no set positions – the lovers just move smoothly from one position to the next without there being any moment when they could be said to be in any one position. The Taoists also recognised the fact that all people, all couples, are physically different and that what one couple can do another may not physically be able to manage, and that there might be false expectations or disappointment if someone couldn't manage something; they might feel that they had somehow 'failed'.

THE TAOIST POSITIONS

The Tao of Loving does describe twenty-six basic positions all of which we have covered; but the Taoists had such interesting names for their positions it's worth looking at a few.

A Phoenix Plays In A Red Cave

The woman, Lady Yin, lies on her back and holds her legs upright with her hands and Lord Yang enters her.

Bamboo Near The Altar

The couple face each other standing up – Intimate Attachment – and the man enters the woman. They can grip on to wherever they feel comfortable.

The Springing White Tiger

The woman kneels forwards and the man kneels behind her. He enters her and she should drop forwards so that her head is touching the ground.

Flying Birds On A Dark Sea

The woman lies on a raised platform or bed with her legs over the side. The man stands and enters her and holds her legs up.

A variation on this is the **Flying Seagull** where the couch or bed is much lower and the man kneels.

Dragon Faces The Mountain

The man sits in a chair and the woman sits in his lap with her back to him.

Dragon Faces The Mountain

The Taoist names

Some of the Taoist terminology is wonderful – we have the 'Jade Hammer', the 'Heavenly Dragon Stem', the 'Red Phoenix', and the 'Coral Stalk' for penis. The 'Jade Pavilion' and 'Palace', the 'Open Lotus Flower', and the 'Red Valley' are for the vulva. The clitoris is the 'Jade Pearl' and the 'Golden Jewel of the Jade Palace'. Sex is 'Mist on the Mountains of Wu', and the 'Meeting of the Dragon and the Unicorn' or even just the 'Clouds and the Rain'. And an orgasm is the 'Bursting of the Clouds'.

So those are the positions. In Chapter 9 we will look at the befores and afters – seduction, erotica, foreplay, intimacy, afterglow and prolonging the mood.

9

THE SPIRITUALITY OF THE EROTIC

A humid kiss is better than a hurried coitus

Old Arab proverb

THE THREE PARTS OF SEX

In the West we tend to divide sex up into three distinct parts: the seduction; the sex; the afterglow. In the East the tantric texts suggest that sex is something that goes on indefinitely – there is no distinction between the three phases; they are all going on all of the time, we just fail to see that. If we hold that in mind our lovemaking becomes even more erotic. Even when we are having sex we should be seducing, arousing, caressing, loving, foreplaying. There will be moments during sex when we will stop to rest and then we can experience the afterglow, but in between instead of at the end. When we are arousing and seducing we can be having sex with our eyes and fingertips. If the energy is universal we can be enjoying any part of it at any time and in any way we want to. The proverb at the beginning of this chapter has its equivalent in Taoism – 'a loving glance from our heart's desire brings us closer to Heaven's rain than a thousand nights of wasted ching'.

A deeper need

The whole point of tantric sexuality is that is promotes sex from being a mere pleasure activity to being one of great spiritual significance. And all the ancient texts agree that spirituality is a twenty-four-hour-a-day pursuit – 'let every act be a service, let every service be worship, let every worship be continuous' (Chu Lin – a Taoist teacher). If sex is a perfect representation of our love not only for our partner but also for the Universal Principle then we should be in love continually. That love can be expressed in a glance, a gesture, a touch, a kiss, a stroke of the hair. These moments are the acts of service, the worship. And they can be as electric as an orgasm. Sometimes we need that love, that closeness to the Universal Principle and we make the mistake of thinking that our need for sex is that love; if we could separate our feelings we might be happier to be close to our lover in a warm and intimate embrace than having quick and unsatisfactory sex. The need for sex is often taken, in the West, for being a need for instant gratification. But there is a deeper need that should be fulfilled. Tantric sex is about using sex to fulfil that deeper need. Our sex life becomes infinitely more varied and exciting if we recognise that we aren't just 'having sex' but also exchanging energy, worshipping the Universal Principle, experiencing an intimacy and closeness with another human being, nurturing our inner self, acting out our karma, and even exploring the universe beyond the confines of our bodies. All in all, quite a package.

If it feels good – do it

In the multipurpose activity of sex, nothing you can do is wrong – providing you are doing it together with mutual consent and participation. In the West there are many barriers to sex and a lot of preconceived notions about what is right or wrong, good or bad, decent or indecent, moral or immoral, nice or not nice, tasteful or distasteful. None of this is true about sex. There is what there is. If it

feels good – do it. If it feels wrong – then don't. Sex can only enhance your spirituality, it can never detract from it. Sex is an act of supreme worship. If the sex is tacky or distasteful, hurried or forbidden, then that is the level of your worship. And remember: 'as you sow so shall you reap'. If your acts of worship are open, loving, relaxed, satisfactory and clear then the Universal Principle will respond in a like manner. If your acts of worship are furtive and guilt-ridden, abusive and badly motivated then how can you expect the Universal Principle to respond positively?

Two notions about sex

There are two notions about sex still prevalent in the West that haven't changed in many hundreds of years. One is that, for men, sex is something to be got in large quantities, and that quality doesn't enter into it. And the other is that for women to enjoy their sexuality openly and freely somehow makes them not nice. Both notions couldn't be further from the truth. But both notions seem to show no signs of departing as rapidly as they should. For men, once they have had it proved that quality is much more important than quantity, they come to realise that sex within a loving, committed, trusting relationship is far more satisfactory and much more sustaining than they would have thought possible. And for women, once they have managed to battle against a thousand hidden social signals that somehow sex is not nice for a woman to enjoy, they come to realise that they are as fully sexually charged as men and entitled to express that sexuality as openly and as freely as they want. 'Men have to learn to step back, women to step forward' – Chu Lin.

Taking the best

Part of the problem with the two notions is that the old tantric texts were written by men, for male dominated societies. We have to take what is best from them and discard the rest – the old, outdated stuff.

We live in a modern, potentially liberated, society where we can explore sexuality in a much freer environment. But we've a long way to go yet.

Making allowances

In this chapter we will look at seduction, erotica, foreplay, intimacy, afterglow and prolonging the mood – and our enjoyment of every one of these is influenced by how far we have come from those two notions. I'm not suggesting that you suffer from either – but your lover may and you have to make allowances.

Seduction

We can wear whatever we like to please our lovers. We can phone them and make suggestive remarks. We can caress them secretly, intimately, in public. We can expose our bodies to our lovers in whatever manner we want. We can take the initiative in suggesting sexual positions or foreplay. We can choose when, where and how we make love.

The important aspects of seduction

How many of the above do you feel comfortable with? It's not a test. Seduction is about getting yourself and your lover ready for making love. It's not about seducing new lovers, that's something different. If you are getting yourself ready you have to think ahead. You have to be considerate and know what your lover likes, wants and needs – and you have to be prepared to give it. That doesn't mean you have to do anything you don't want to, or find objectionable or distasteful. It means you have to be considerate of your lover's sexual needs and proclivities; and your own, of course. You have to know how you respond to each other sexually – and this all means communication. If you don't talk about it you won't know. If you

don't pick up the signals you'll remain in the dark. The three most important aspects of seduction are: atmosphere, idea and inclination.

The right atmosphere

You have to provide the right atmosphere. The room for making love should be prepared in advance – and if your dream is to have savage and wonderfully wanton sex on the kitchen table (and yes, you are allowed to; under the rule of tantric sex anything you want is permissible) then you might need to clear away the dirty dishes and make sure the table is sturdy enough. There are many couples whose lovemaking goes wildly astray through lack of planning.

The idea

We have to implant the idea. A whispered suggestion can be more seductive than an open invitation because most sex goes on in the lover's head. The idea is very important. A tiny hint of what is to come later is a bit like reading the menu in a restaurant – it whets the appetite and gets the juices flowing.

The inclination

The inclination has to be there. If you provide the first two then the third will undoubtedly follow. If it doesn't you can help it along by knowing your partner's needs. If your partner is never very sexy first thing in the morning and you want desperately to make love when you are half waking up then you could always suggest an afternoon nap (or whatever time your lover is particularly 'in the mood'). You'll get your wish and your lover will be happy to oblige without having to force anything. Plan ahead and use what you know about each other to satisfy both of you.

Erotica

The Japanese *Shunga* or 'spring drawings' as well as the Chinese 'pillow books' contain explicit pictures of people making love in all sorts of positions and places. And they are very erotic. They were designed to help couples know what was available and how to participate. They weren't designed to titillate or provide single males with fantasies. They were for couples.

The centrefold syndrome

Modern erotica falls woefully short of the sophistication of the Japanese and Chinese drawings. Recent research done at the University of California by Dr Deborah Then has highlighted a modern condition – the 'centrefold syndrome'. This is where men become dissatisfied with their partners because they don't look like *Playboy* centrefolds. Unfortunately, centrefolds are not 'normal': they have had breast implants, substantial 'air-brushing' and myriad other tweaks and tricks of the trade to make them more glamorous and 'sexy'. But it can make men feel unhappy with real women – 75 per cent of the men questioned by Dr Then said that they wanted the women in their lives to look like centrefolds. And many said that because they didn't, it caused problems.

God's a bit fat, too

Because of the vast amounts of pornography, men's magazines and such like that are available today in the West, men may all be unconsciously guilty of the centrefold syndrome to a greater or lesser extent. And the same seems to be happening to women. They too suffer from a need for their partners to have the 'Calvin Klein look'. If your lover is a perfect representation of the Universal Principle then perhaps you just have to accept that the Universal Principle has wobbly bits!

foreplay

The whispered suggestion that we mentioned under seduction is the start of foreplay. Good foreplay is as important as good sex – it's providing the atmosphere, the idea and the inclination. Too often it's rushed as if it's something to be got through before the main course. But it can be the main course.

Once we lose the Western orgasm/goal focus we can enjoy foreplay until it becomes all play. How many lovers have you known who, as soon as penetrative sex takes place, stop tweaking and touching all those sensitive bits that they were touching beforehand? How many lovers think that a quick bit of fondling will 'get them in the mood'? How wrong are they? Foreplay should be continuous throughout sex – and afterwards. Foreplay is all the best bits – the licking and kissing, the fondling and caressing, the touching and stroking, the tasting and nibbling, the smelling and teasing, the rubbing and scratching, the tweaking and biting, the sucking and rousing. Need I say more?

Intimacy

Sex is the closest we will ever get to each other: inside each other and around each other. If we trust another to be that close we have to be *intimate* with each other. The word intimate comes from the Latin *intermatum* – 'within'. And that's where we should be with our lovers – within. Within their hearts and minds and souls. That's the beauty of tantric sexuality – it teaches us about respect. And when we respect the person we are making love with then we can be truly intimate because we trust each other with our inner selves as well. Then we can let go and be truly open. When we are intimate with our lovers we are opening ourselves not only to them but also to that energy, that Universal Principle. Then we can be filled with that energy. If we are closed we cannot receive anything.

Afterglow

After sex, afterglow. That is the time for warmth and companionship, for holding and being close to our lover. Not for getting up and going off to watch TV, or for falling asleep, or for going home to our spouse. Afterglow is for bathing in, for recharging the energy, for holding and comforting, for re-establishing ourselves in that love, for getting our breath back so we are ready again to please our lover, for enjoying our lover's satisfaction and contentment. Afterglow is for glowing in afterwards. Don't hurry it, enjoy it.

Prolonging the mood

The Taoists say that if you let the fires of sexual energy dwindle too low then you have to relight them all over again – but if you blow on the embers, the fire will flare up again quickly. During the afterglow you can continue caressing and touching and then you will prolong the mood. And then the afterglow will become seduction, and the seduction foreplay, and your sexuality will be continuous – and you'll be truly tantric.

Homosexual tantric sex

If you are in a gay relationship please feel free to adopt any of the principles in this book for your own sexuality. The tantric texts didn't cover gay sex to a great extent; however any two people who are in a loving, trusting relationship can practise tantric sex, no matter what sex they are. Tantric sex is about using sex as a means of enhancing our spirituality, and that Universal Principle embraces all of us no matter what path we followed to get there.

final word

This is a book in the *Beginner's guide* series. Please feel free to follow up this wide and varied subject. I have recommended some books in the Useful Information section which comes next. Modern translations of all the ancient texts are available: some of them are pretty hard going. And there are courses and workshops you can attend if you wish. Remember, however, that you can only learn by practice; no books or courses are going to teach you anything nearly as well as a considerate, caring, patient lover. And you can be your lover's teacher, too. Sex may seem to be a serious subject but it's not really; sex is about having fun and enjoyment; about opening yourself up to pleasure as the greatest embodiment of human satisfaction; about reunion with the fundamental energy of the universe; about taking part in the richness and excitement of being alive. And it's all free. Having sex is being rich.

Two minutes

By the way, research has shown that the *average* time for sex, in the West, is two minutes – and that's everything: foreplay, penetrative sex, afterglow. By practising some of the techniques and exercises described in this book we might be able to improve on that two minutes.

USEFUL INFORMATION

Suggested Further Reading

An Introduction to Asian Religions, E. G. Parrinder, SPCK, 1958.
Anne Hooper's Kama Sutra, Anne Hooper, Dorling Kindersley, 1994.
Chakras for Beginners, Naomi Ozaniec, Hodder & Stoughton, 1995.
Chinese Horoscopes for Beginners, Kristyna Arcarti, Hodder & Stoughton, 1995.
Erotic Art of the East, Philip Rawson, Weidenfeld & Nicolson, 1973.
Exotic Massage for Lovers, Timothy Freke, An Eddison Sadd Edition, 1996.
Fundamentals of Human Sexuality, Herant A. Katchadourian and Donald T. Lunde, Holt, Rinehart & Winston, Inc, 1972.
Sex in History, Reay Tannahill, Sphere Books, 1990.
Sexual Awareness, Barry & Emily McCarthy, Headline Books, 1991.
Sexual Energy Ecstasy, David & Ellen Ramsdale, Bantam Books, 1991.
Sky Dancer, Keith Dowman, Routledge & Kegan Paul, 1984.
Tantra: The Art of Conscious Loving, Charles and Caroline Muir, Mercury House, 1989.
Tantra: The Key to Sexual Power and Pleasure, Ashley Thirleby, Dell, 1978.
Tantra: the Yoga of Sex, Omar Garrison, Avon Books, 1973.
Tantric Sex, E. J. Gold, Peak Skill Publishing, 1988.
Tantric Sex, Robert Moffett, Berkely Medallion, 1974.

The Clouds and the Rain: the Art of Love in China, Michael Beurdeley, H. Hammond, 1969.

The Illustrated Kama Sutra of Vatsyayana, translated by Sir Richard Burton, Fraser Stewart Books, 1992.

The Kama Sutra, translated by Sir Richard Burton, Panther Books, 1963.

The Mythology of Sex, Sarah Denning, Batsford Books, 1996.

The Perfumed Garden of the Shaykh Nefzawi, translated by Sir Richard Burton, Panther Books, 1963.

The Sensual Touch, Dr Glenn Wilson, MacDonald Orbis, 1989.

The Spiritual Traditions of Sex, Richard Craze, Godsfield Press, 1996.

The Tantric Way, Ajit Mookerjee and Madhu Khanna, New York Graphic Society, 1977.

The Tao of Health, Sex, and Longevity, Daniel Reid, Fireside, 1989.

The Tao of Love, Jolan Chang, Wildwood House Ltd, 1977.

The Tao of Sex, Akira Ishihira and Howard Levy, Integral Publishing, 1989.

Yoga, Ernest Wood, Penguin Books, 1959.

Internet Addresses

Guide to Tantric Sex: Beginner's Guide to Tantra
http://www.widemedia.com/annual/tantric.html

Books: Tantric Sex Positions
http://www.lovepotion.com/books/B5001-00.html

Better Sex: Tantric Sex Education
http://www.greatsex.com

Tantric Sex: A Spiritual Path of Ecstasy
http://www.tantra.org/virato.htm

The Pictorial Guide to Tantric Sex
http://www.cl.ais.net/jestor1/order.html

Courses

United Kingdom

Introductory evenings, days and weekends for beginners in tantra. Year-long training in Love, Sexuality and Partnership for couples. Training in Love and Ecstasy for singles and couples. Tantric celebrations and rituals. Write to:

John Hawken
Skydancing UK
Lower Grunbla Farm
Newbridge
Penzance
Cornwall
TR20 8QX

Information and programmes:
Louise Maingard
Skydancing Institute UK
47 Maple Road
Horfield
Bristol
BS7 8RE

USA

Seminars, courses and sacred sexuality products; educational books; audio and visual tapes; practical courses on sexual healing, erotic massage, loving relationships, men's liberation; advanced week-long retreats. Write to:

Attn: Manager
Peak Skill
PO Box 5489
Playa del Rey
CA 90296

The Aspen Group
PO Box 2677
Aspen
CO 81672

Sacred sexuality seminars
Dr Stephen Chang
Tao Academy
2700 Ocean Avenue
San Francisco
CA 94132

Source retreats
Box 69
Paia
Maui
HI 96779

Kundalini workshops
The Kundalini Clinic
Oakland
CA

Spiritual Emergence Centre
1010 Doyle
Suite 10
Menlo Park
CA 94025

Advanced sex education
National Sex Forum
1523 Franklin Street
San Francisco
CA 94109

Kahua Institute
Box 1747
Makawao
Maui
HI 96768

Sensuality training
Secret Garden
1352 Yukon Way
20 Novato
CA 94947

Dhyanyoga Centre
Box 3194
Antioch
CA 94531

**Kinsey Institute for Research in
Sex, Gender and Reproduction**
Indiana University
Morrison Hall
Bloomington
Indiana 47405

India

Bihar School of Tantric Yoga
Monghyr 811201
Bihar

Thapas Yoga Ashram
5 Rathas Road
Mahabalipuram

Sri Lakshmana Ashram
Chillakur
Gudur
Nellore Dist 524412
Andhra Pradesh

Sri Ramanasramam
Tiruvannamalai 606 603

Sweden

Swami Janakananda
Scandinavian Yoga and Meditation Centre
S-340 13 Hamneda

Switzerland

The Skydancing Institute
37 Geeringstrasse
8049 Zurich

Hawaii

Art of being
PO Box 38
Paia
Hawaii 96779